HIGHLY EFFECTIVE QUESTIONING

CHALLENGING THE CULTURE OF DISENGAGEMENT IN THE K-12 CLASSROOM

FIFTH EDITION, April, 2006©

EDITORS

Percival Matthews, M.A., Editor

Nicholas Krump, B.A., Editor

It's been nearly ten years since I first began work in the area of oral classroom questioning based upon the initial efforts of my parents, Drs. Lee and Veronica Hannel. Over this time, I have grown in my own understanding of the issues associated with using oral classroom questioning as a core way of teaching. I must thank our audiences of teachers, our company's trainers, friends abroad, classes of students throughout the world, and all those interested in how questioning can improve teaching for the insights I have learned from them.

Here, let me share some of my most recent reflections with you about our work in Highly Effective Questioning, hereafter HEQ throughout this book.

The first idea is that, unfortunately, most K-12 teachers continue to lack training in how to use intensive oral questioning in the classroom as the basis for part of their instruction. That this is so remains puzzling, given that questioning is one of the very ways in which to communicate—and thus teach—another person. There are of course other ways of teaching, such as via lecture (tell), modeling (show), exploration (experience) and experiment (test). But questioning is important enough to constitute its own unique way of teaching. It deserves study.

What proportion of teachers would say that they have been given true training—not just a few 'hints' or suggestions or lists of verb-stems or "remember Bloom's Taxonomy"—about how to question students effectively and intensely? My own experience suggests that fewer than 1 in 10 teachers would say that they have been trained in how to question students in a substantial way.

The second idea is that because of this lack of training, most educators rely on intuition as to how to question students. For those teachers who were infrequently questioned when they were students, it is natural to imitate or revert to what is more familiar such as lecture or task-based activities. To sit around and ask questions in a systematic way is what feels unnatural.

Reliance on intuition has left several interesting artifacts of the ineffective or inefficient use of questioning in the classroom. An obvious one is that many students simply don't like to be questioned, as they grow older. Why does that have to be so? It doesn't. The culture of disengagement is what takes over when oral classroom questioning is left to intuition.

The third idea is that students who have reduced capacities for oral communication will find the consequences more debilitating as time goes on. This is not just to say the manifest, such as that intensive oral questioning improves self-explanation, which improves understanding or that it corresponds with success on test questions or that it encourages classroom engagement.

Consider a second perspective. Imagine a world in which there are many, multitudes, literally a plethora of brilliant people from which to choose. Imagine that you can't swing a stick without hitting an excellent student, competent engineer, or a strong researcher. What would help you distinguish amongst the many competent students or job candidates when so many are similar in underlying skill? The premium, perhaps the make it or break it factor, will be how well the person is able to talk or communicate with you. Students who don't like to be questioned are in for a rough road.

There is a window of opportunity to turn around the culture of disengagement in American classrooms and encourage our students to learn the power of their own voices. But if they do not learn to speak, I imagine that others will speak in their stead, perhaps in Chinese or Hindi or even English but in other places.

About this book itself. You will notice the absence of references or citations to others' work in this book and in previous editions of HEQ. This is an outcome both inadvertent and purposeful. It is inadvertent because when I first began this work in 1995, I wasn't familiar with what others had written about critical thinking or questioning strategies. An attorney by training, I didn't bring an educational background or perspective to the creation of HEQ. To be honest, I didn't even bring an attorney's perspective, as the classroom is substantially different than the courtroom. In short, HEQ was and is in many respects an original work.

I am sometimes asked why I don't cite other authors or endeavor now to find, in the vagaries of journals of education, support for the ideas of HEQ. To be blunt, the outcomes or effectiveness of those ideas have already been felt—or better put, not felt. For instance, Bloom's Taxonomy is well known and there is evidence that indeed the mind builds information in a hierarchical way. And HEQ accords with Bloom's Taxonomy in most respects. However, Bloom's Taxonomy has been around for nearly half a century and still little change has occurred in the ways teachers question students. It occurs to me to ask why one should seek validation from that which has not resonated with teachers in a practical way? Maybe a changed approach or—more likely—a changed explanation is needed.

What HEQ offers is less compliance with or divergence from other ideas or practices about questioning. I will leave you, the reader, to interpret where HEQ is familiar or inconsonant. Rather, what HEQ offers is a different way of explaining ideas about questioning in the K-12 classroom. HEQ, then, is not a "program" but more of a description how questioning can improve understanding—a way of thinking. In my mind, HEQ discusses questioning in the same way another book might discuss storytelling or lecture.

In HEQ workshops, however, we go beyond simply explaining things. Each workshop we do has a live student demonstration with students using grade level content. For all the merits of other critical thinking/ questioning strategies, HEQ can be literally seen in action, not just heard in theory.

I think the failure of questioning strategies to take hold in classrooms is less about particular methodologies than about teachers having a deep resonance with the ideas or metaphors used to describe effective questioning. And that is what I hope this book brings you, new ideas or old ideas put in a new way.

I hope you find HEQ useful to your own efforts with students. As with any set of ideas, the classroom teacher is the one who has to use judgment in the application of HEQ and know when to use, bend, or break the suggestions provided in this book. I encourage you in all respects and am always available for questions, comments, and thoughts.

Ivan Hannel, J.D.
Phoenix, Arizona, United States of America
January 2006
Email: contact@hannel.com

CHAPTER ONE:

DEFINING A
CRITICAL THINKING SKILL

The very first order of business in learning how to question effectively is to consider why we question students in the first place. Why are we questioning students? Many educators, indeed, many people would say to develop "critical thinking skills" or "critical thinking" or something to that effect.

And that makes sense. We aren't questioning just to hear ourselves asking questions. We, as teachers, question students in order to make them think at the moment but also, somehow, to get them to develop their own processes or mechanisms or patterns of thinking.

Unfortunately, the term 'critical thinking skills' is not self-defining. So, we have to give it some concrete definition because if we are asking students questions for the purpose of developing these critical thinking skills, then we must have some way of discerning what engages critical thinking skills and what does not. Is asking a student, "What is the sum of 2 + 2?" a 'critical thinking skills' question? Is asking a student, "Can you put the information in order?" a critical thinking skills question? In short, let us make an attempt to define the elements of what makes something a critical thinking skill—and worth questioning about—or something different.

In HEQ, we have defined a critical thinking skill as having four key elements or parts. In order for something to be a critical thinking skill, it must be:
• A mental act
• Mentally intensive
• Generalizable across content areas
• Amenable to instruction

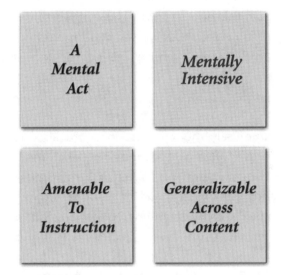

Mental Act

A critical thinking skill must be a mental act. This is simply to say that it is an activity of the mind. The idea that a critical thinking skill is a kind of mental activity is very powerful. It allows us to believe that most students can engage in critical thinking. We can "trigger" through our questions certain kinds of mental acts, the ones we will define as meeting all four elements of critical thinking skills. Thus, critical thinking is a conventional thing, something to be expected of most people and students who have functional brains.

The definition of critical thinking as being a very conventional or common set of mental acts that most people can do contrasts with some educators' perceptions of what is critical thinking. These people associate critical thinking less with mental acts and more with abstract qualities like inventiveness or creativity or with people who exemplify the same (e.g., Einstein or Bill Gates).

The problem with such associations is that anything short of "creative thought" is denigrated as not being critical thinking. And a tendency of people who define critical thinking as creative thought is that they often fail to perceive that creative types are normally quite accomplished in more conventional ways, too. That is, creative people normally can do the basic activities or answer basic questions about a task or in a field as well as answer more complicated, perhaps even novel ones.

When "creative" questions become the definition of critical thinking, we run into some problems. For instance, if one were to ask an engineer to develop a rather conventional bridge, whose basic design is well known, does that mean that the engineer is not thinking critically because his design is not completely novel? Is the heart surgeon who completes his 50th routine bypass not thinking critically?

In HEQ, critical thinking is a set of commonplace mental acts. We elicit those mental acts through questions. The more often or intensely the student's mental acts are triggered in certain patterns, the more likely the student will develop the full range of critical thinking skills. Critical thinking, then, is not the outcome of some process of thought but the process of thought itself.

One of the incidental benefits of defining critical thinking as certain kinds of mental acts is that it suggests that we can develop these skills using all kinds of content. We can ask students questions about a common newspaper article and develop critical thinking skills. We can ask students questions about their daily experience and develop critical thinking skills. We can ask students questions about a passage or problem from a state test and still be developing their critical thinking skills. Thus, what we question students about—its topicality or inherent interest--is less important than about how we question them (to elicit mental acts). Activities, then, that are not "exciting" or "brilliant"' or "creative" can be just fine for developing critical thinking skills—up to a point which we will talk about next.

Mentally Intensive

If critical thinking skills are fundamentally mental acts, then are all kinds of mental acts critical thinking skills? The answer, I believe, is no. Certain kinds of questions may elicit mental acts but do so with a low level of mental intensity. Asking a student a question like, "What is 5 multiplied by 7?" is not mentally intensive enough to be considered an act of critical thinking. In education-ese, we might say that such a question could be answered merely by "recall" or is just a knowledge-level question. But I don't think that describing "What is 5 multiplied by 7?" as merely a recall question, tells us exactly why it should not considered as a question that develops critical thinking.

All questions that engage what is not immediately on the mind require recall. To say that a question only requires recall is to say the obvious, which is that almost all questions require some degree of remembering. The reason that "What is 5 multiplied by 7?" is not mentally intensive has nothing to do with recall or remembering. It has to do with the fact that the connection established between 5 sets of 7 things, whose sum is 35, has been asked so often that most students no longer need exert mental effort to answer the question.

By comparison, consider that asking an adult to speak their home address is usually very easily answered but asking a young child to answer the same question might require a much greater effort at connecting the descriptors of the address with the location sought. The child knows his home but doesn't connect the verbal descriptions of it with the place he goes to sleep. For the adult, no thinking is required because the association is so strong. For the child, the association is simply not as strong, and that rather than the idea of recall explains why the child can't "remember" his address. It's not about forgetting; it's about a weaker connection between two sets of information.

As teachers in the classroom, we often can intuit which questions require more mental effort and thus critical thinking than others. Questions to develop critical thinking must pass some threshold of intensity. Thus, a question like "What is 5 multiplied by 7?" may be an all too familiar associative question to require mentally intensive thought. But another common question like "What is the main idea?" may require significant mental exertion to answer. So, in formulating critical thinking skills questions, we should bear in mind the degree of mental intensity the questions require.

Generalizable Across Content

Within every area of content, there are specific kinds of activities that are unique and important to understanding. In calculus, we might need to take a derivative or in chemistry we might need to apply a rule of significant figures or in poetry we might look to find an instance of alliteration. Every content area will eventually have its own ever-narrowing set of mental activities that one might argue is an example of critical thinking. Eventually, though, such a definition would make it hard to differentiate the mental acts of critical thinking from very narrow mental acts within one's field of study.

So, one requirement of the mental acts of critical thinking is that they can be used or applied to several content areas. I can't ask you to "take a derivative" in a short story, so that mental activity, though it requires many mental acts of critical thinking, is not itself a critical thinking skill. Oppositely, I can ask you to identify the terms of a derivative or the rules of significant figures or the words that seem to have repeating consonants in a poem. Thus, the mental act of identifying is a generalizable across content area but "taking a derivative" is not.

Amenable to Instruction

The final element of the definition of a critical thinking skill is that it be something that can be taught. A critical thinking skill must be a mental act whose acuity can be enhanced. If, for instance, I ask you to make many comparisons of characters in novels, you will likely become better at making comparisons of characters in novels. Your responses—your thinking—will become more complete and fluid and interesting in that capacity. Critical thinking, then, is not the acuity you have due to some genetic twist of fate, but the skills you develop over time from repeated teaching and learning experiences that activate certain mental acts.

CHAPTER TWO:

THE TRIANGLE
OF THE THREE C'S

Since we have just defined what a critical thinking skill is, it is important to establish how the development of these particular mental skills helps the student to become more intelligent. How do the ability to identify, to compare, to sequence and other critical thinking skills develop "understanding" in students?

In fact, what does understanding mean? For most educators, we associate understanding with having students know something at the conceptual level. A concept is defined as "an abstract or general idea inferred or derived from specific instances" according to The American Heritage Dictionary. We might also use a synonym of the word rule to define the idea of concept.

So, how do critical thinking skills—these particular mental acts—lead to conceptual or rule-making skills in students?

According to HEQ, we have a framework called "The Triangle of the 3 Cs" that explains the interrelationship between the development of critical thinking skills, content, and understanding at a conceptual level.

The framework says this: Through the repeated exercise of one's critical thinking skills according to particular patterns within a body of content, the student eventually will develop understanding at a conceptual level.

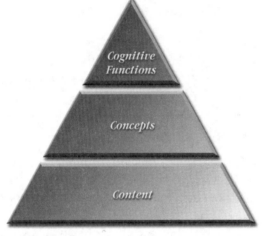

Below are two examples that may help to make clear how The Triangle of the 3 Cs operates.

Example 1
The first example requires you to write out three numbers on a sheet of paper.
- One thousand seven hundred and seventy-six
- One thousand nine hundred and forty-one
- One thousand eight hundred and sixty-one

Before you read the explanation of this example, please answer each of the following questions:
- After you have written these numbers out, what do you notice?
- Are the numbers just quantities or something else?
- How are they the same or different?
- What do they all have in common?
- Did you notice that they were given out of order?
- What is the theme to this content?

The first step for most people in the process of understanding this small body of content is to translate the written language into numerical form so that they can be seen as numbers. Some of you may have written out the following:

1,776   1,941   1,861

Then, perhaps you noticed that the numbers had something in common? Through a pattern of association or connection, you might see that the numbers were really dates representing the Revolutionary War, World War II, and the Civil War.

1776   1941   1861

You might even have put them in a more normal order in your own mind, as they proceed along a timeline:

1776   1861   1941

When asked, "How are they the same or different" or "What do they all have in common," you may have gone further and began to make subtler distinctions. They were all wars but different kinds of wars: revolutionary, international, and civil.

And when asked, "What themes come to mind," you might have considered the larger ideas or concepts of war, freedom, sacrifice, conflict and so on.

Now, let's analyze what you did when given the initial three pieces of content. You labeled and identified, then you connected and compared, and finally you put things in order and began to see the content as a whole. You may have done these mental acts automatically or as a function of the written questions that triggered you to see the information in a new way.

The key here is to understand that critical thinking skills—the ability to identify, connect, compare and so forth—help us to make enough connections between things so that we can rise in our understanding to "concepts." As adults, when we are given new information, we go through a process of exercising our critical thinking skills almost subconsciously or automatically.

But not all learners engage in this process as fluidly or independently. Asking oral questions can help the student learner exercise his or her critical thinking skills and provide the tactical engagement needed for the student to rise in understanding to the conceptual level.

Example 2
Below is a list of content. See what you can make from the content and put that in the space provided:

1. Eggs   _____
2. Eggs, Sugar   _____
3. Eggs, Sugar, Flour   _____
4. Eggs, Sugar, Flour, Chocolate _____

I am no baker. But when I see the first line of "eggs," I do not think "cake" or "chocolate chip cookies." That is more of what I think of when I look at line 4. This brief example helps us to see that when given certain content, we exercise our critical thinking skills and come up with different concepts almost automatically.

Construction v. Exposure to Concepts

There is an interesting and important implication from The Triangle of the 3 Cs.

Concepts are ideas or rules or themes are "built up" by the repeated exercise of the learner's cognitive functions, according to certain patterns, within and upon a body of content. Concepts are not things that can be given as a whole to students, in the specific sense that you can't just tell students a rule and expect understanding from that. For instance, simply telling students that $E = mc^2$ or that $a^2 + b^2 = c^2$ is not enough. Students must be engaged in the identification, connection, and integration of the elements of the rule and then to particular sets of facts in order for understanding to occur.

Some teachers believe that a failure to understand things at a conceptual level is because students have failed to have enough exposure or experience of seeing something done over and over to understand it. So students are made to repeatedly observe or experience something in the hopes that eventually they will understand it.

The point of views that mere exposure or presentation of a process or concept will succeed in teaching it to the student contrasts with HEQ. The difference is that in HEQ, the student is made responsible for every element of identification, connection, ordering and other cognitive acts of a process or concept. Through our many questions, we make students piece together and repeatedly connect in larger chunks the entirety of a concept. We do not go forward with a presentation of a concept to completion in the hope that the students will, by observation or experience alone, learn the whole concept.

A metaphor might help. Imagine you were teaching someone to build a house. In HEQ, we question the students through each step of the task. The first step of the building of a house might be to select land and then to make a foundation. We ask questions about that. A subsequent step might be to make a frame. We ask questions about that and how it is connected to the first step of selecting the land. A third step might be to create a roof. We ask questions about that and how that is related to the supporting frame and the foundation. In HEQ, we question the student through each step of the process and have them connect it all together. By contrast, someone might simply demonstrate the process of making a house from foundation to frame to roof and expect the student to understand how it's done.

Where does this difference in perspective about the "construction" of concepts versus the "exposure" to concepts come from? I believe it is because, as trained learners, most adults operate at the conceptual level without having to revisit each step of the cognitive process consciously in doing a task. You might say we operate on autopilot.

For example, consider how an adult looks at a car and how a child looks at a car. The adult looks at an object and thinks, "car." But before doing so, we have automatically looked at the attributes of the object and identified key parts. If we notice two tires per side of a vehicle, you think "car" or possibly "motorcycle." If you were to see three tires on a side, you'd probably think truck or something else. We compare the proportions of the vehicle from front to middle and middle to back. This comparison dictates whether the vehicle is a car or a station wagon or a truck. All of this cognition occurs at once. We aren't even aware of it.

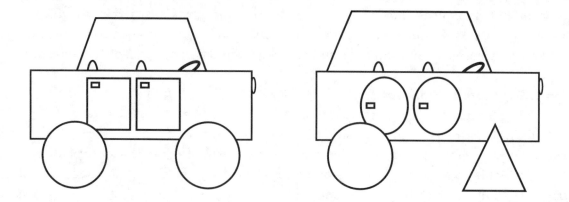

The child, by contrast, must often be taught exactly how to look at an object before rising to the level of classification of "car." The car is often first a "train" before it becomes a car, because the attention to detail or parts must be made explicit. In HEQ, we ask questions to help the student construct a concept from the lowest levels of cognition to the highest.

A final metaphor might help. Imagine a person who comes from a foreign place and knows nothing about the game of basketball. When he is placed in the game without an understanding of the ball, the players, the allowed movements or the sequences of play, he may become frustrated in his understanding. Yes, eventually, after seeing enough games of basketball played or perhaps playing in them, he'll eventually get the feel of it. But compare that process to having a coach break the game into each different components, from identifying the players to connecting movements to organizing plays, and you can imagine which method produces a stronger and more confident player.

CHAPTER THREE:

WHY ASK QUESTIONS

Why Ask Questions

In previous chapters, we have learned the definition of a critical thinking skill and how those skills lead to the development of conceptual understandings. The next hurdle is to learn why questioning strategies are particularly important to that process. In short, why ask questions?

One way of understanding the need for questioning is to outline the means of communication available to the classroom teacher. Along with content knowledge, the act of teaching is at heart an act of communication. Can I get you to understand what I already know or see something both of us must learn? Teaching is communication.

Without going into every niche of communication, we can outline the common ways of teaching as telling (lecture), modeling (showing), experience, experiment (testing/hypothesis) and questioning. Beyond this list, it's hard to find truly different or new kinds of communication. Yes, there are other means of communication, such as storytelling or what have you, but the broad categories listed encompass most recognized communication strategies.

Questioning, then, is one of the very few commonly available means of communication with a class of students. It has often occurred to me that there are more ways to transfer information from one computer to another than one person to another. Questions are a key transfer or discovery mechanism of information from the teacher to the learner.

Assessment

Asking questions helps us to assess, on a moment-by-moment basis, what students presently know. Contrast this with lecture. Usually, in lecture, minutes may go by before students are either asked to give feedback or volunteer feedback without prompting. Certainly, gaps in the stream-of-information that comes via lecture or even independent reading are less likely to occur when questions are being asked regularly.

New Learning Moments

Asking questions goes beyond finding out what students already know or don't know. Indeed, we could find out much the same information using written questions via quizzes. It turns out that asking the right question, with the proper phrasing and in a certain order, can lead students to new moments of learning. So, oral questions both tell us what the student already knows and help to trigger the mental acts needed to identify a missing element, connect two things together, outline the steps of a process—to make mental leaps in learning.

Improving Teachers' Understanding

Questioning is also beneficial in improving the way we, as teachers, understand a lesson. Questioning forces us to take the perspective of the learner much more so than via lecture, modeling, or other kinds of teaching. When we ask questions, we will get many more incorrect or undesired responses if we are not considering how the student perceives the information at hand.

Consider the following common situation. Have you ever been driving with someone as they explained a particular route and then, after having completed it, they ask, "Okay, so you can get here by yourself, right?" Or have you ever had someone show you a multi-step problem or recipe and then turn to you and say, "Got it?" The learner's answer, which I think we often suppress for reasons of pride, should truly be, "I lost you a while ago." But from the teacher's perspective, everything seems like the student should know it, as I showed

CHAPTER THREE: WHY ASK QUESTIONS

it to you step-by-step.

Now, take the teacher's perspective one more time. Except this time, you aren't allowed to show the person how to get to the house or make that recipe. Instead, you are trying to teach how to find some file on your computer or make some recipe, but this time you can only talk to him or her over the phone.

Which method, talking via the phone or modeling—requires more understanding on the part of the teacher? Via the phone, you have to ask a lot more questions and really discover how the learner is trying to understand something. What are the learner's basic perceptions? What do they see as connected? What do they SEE?

This way of teaching by asking questions can be more frustrating from the teacher's perspective than explanation in person or showing something at hand. It is a lot harder to do. But mentally, asking questions puts the burden of the mental work squarely upon the student. And asking questions forces us as teachers to see things much more from the student's perspective than via other communication methods.

Engagement of Reluctant Learners

In the past, if I were asked to establish a hierarchy of the important reasons for asking questions, perhaps the idea of "engagement" would be in the second or third position after creating new learning moments and improving teachers' understandings. Now, I believe that engagement is itself the critical reason for asking questions. I will leave to a different book a more complete explanation of how questions help to challenge what I call "The Culture of Disengagement."

Think about your school for a moment. Can some students can go part of a day, a whole day, several days or heaven's forbid longer without having to answer academic questions? Part of the reason for asking questions is that it forces the involvement of students who do not want to participate in school. There is a difference, of course, between students who may momentarily need a second to think or relax and who might want to be "skip a question" and those students who seemingly always want to be skipped over. Questioning strategies help us to engage the true reluctant learner, of which there seems to be many in schools nowadays.

CHAPTER FOUR:

PHRASING OF QUESTIONS

One topic that is often brought up in workshops is how to phrase the questions we ask students. How should we phrase our questions? An even better starting point is how does phrasing impact the degree of learning done by the student?

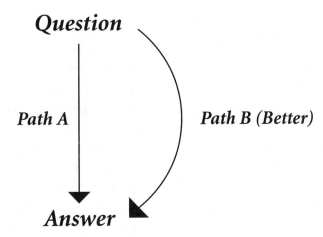

The way a question is phrased matters because it determines the amount of mental work that is available for the student to do. According to HEQ, the more mental work that a question allows, the better the question's phrasing is. As seen above, Path B is better because it is longer. While both questions get to the Answer, Path B requires more (mental) work and is thus a better question. How might we determine whether a particular question will require more or less mental work? There are two terms to describe whether a particular question's phrasing will require more or less mental work. The terms are "scope" and "intentionality."

Scope

If the potential answer-set to a question is broad or deep, then we might say that the scope of the question is good. Consider a question like, "Do you see X?" The scope of the question is very narrow. The question limits the breadth of possible answers to X, a single thing. The question also isn't very deep, in the sense that it triggers what is mostly perceived as a lower-order thinking skill, the mental act of identification. So, to assess the scope of a question we consider both the availability of justifiable answers and the degree of thinking required to answer it.

Let's look at a similar question that is better in its scope: "What do you see?" In this case, the question again requires identification, so it still triggers a lower order thinking skill. However, the answer set to the question is potentially very large. If there are many things to be noticed, then the question might require significant mental effort to answer it properly.

A question like, "What are several things you can infer from the story?" is even better in its scope. Why? First, it requires that several things be inferred. The answer set to the question is at least "several things." Second, the question is deeper because it requires the mental act of inference, which is higher in the order of thinking skills, as you'll soon read.

To summarize the concept of scope, a question's scope is determined both by the quantity of answers it may elicit (how broad is it?) and the kind of mental activity needed to answer it (how deep is it?).

But the effectiveness of a question is not determined solely by what is asks. We also must consider the quality of the student's response to it. As teachers, we can phrase our questions in ways that should elicit mentally demanding answers, but if students feel that any response will do, little understanding will be developed.

Intentionality

In HEQ, we use the term "intentionality" to describe how to evaluate and develop students' responses, so that our inquiries prompt the desired growth in understanding. Intentionality can be thought of as our "intention" (or goal or purpose) behind asking a particular question. There are three criteria by which we evaluate a student's response to a question: (1) specificity, (2) completeness, and (3) justification. Is the student's response specific, complete, and justified?

Specificity means, do I know exactly what the student is talking about? Completeness means, has the student shown me all the parts of the response that I'd like to hear about? And justification means, is there evidence or reasoning behind what is being said (per Principle 4)? Again, no matter how well-phrased our initial questions may be, the efficacy of a question is also determined by the way in which the student responds to it.

Timeline: What are the most important events on the timeline?

P	X	Q	Y	A	Z	D	C

Student Response: "I see three important events."
Student Response: "I see X and Y."
Student Response: "I think X, Y and Z are the most important."

Example: Phrasing of Questions

Let's look at how the ideas of scope and intentionality work together in the actual practice of a asking a question. Imagine I ask some students, "What the three key events on the timeline provided?" First, let's analyze the scope of the question. Is it broad? Well, there are three components to the desired answer, so that's probably fairly broad. Is it a deep question? As we'll see, it requires identification of events and probably some comparison to ensure that they are "key" events. So, it might be a deeper or higher order kind of question.

Assume the intended response to the question is for the student to select dates X, Y, and Z as the three key events on the timeline. Rather than saying, "I think X, Y, and Z are the three key dates because of these reasons," student Jim says, "I see three key dates." Why doesn't Jim's answer meet our intentionality? Let's look to our criteria. Is it specific, justified, and complete?

The answer is not specific because we don't know which exact dates Jim is referring to. The answer may be complete because Jim refers to three dates he has found. But the response shows no clear reason(s) as to why Jim chose X, Y, and Z. Jim's overall response is not what we intended to hear; it does not meet our intentionality. We might have to ask several follow-up questions at this point, beginning with, "Why did you select those three dates, Jim?"

What if Alice says, "I think that X and Y are the most important dates because each shows a turning point from states' rights to a more federalist system." The response is specific in its identification of X and Y. The response seems to have some justification or reasoning, too. The response is still incomplete, however, and so the teacher might need to follow up, "Alice, is there another date that fits with X and Y, too?"

And finally, imagine Percy says, "I select X, Y, and Z because all have that federalist…uh, yeah, they are just the right ones." The student is specific and complete, but the justification seems confused. The teacher might ask, "Percy, could you tell me more about your reasoning in selecting X, Y and X?"

In sum, the phrasing of questions affects the degree of mental work that is open or available to students to enact via their responses. Questions that are narrow in scope preclude the student from answering in a way that triggers strong mental activity. Even when the question is phrased properly, it is important that students' responses be specific, justified and complete in order to meet the intention behind a question.

CHAPTER FIVE:

CREATING AN ATTITUDE OF ENGAGEMENT —
THE SEVEN PRINCIPLES OF HIGH EXPECTATIONS

Creating an Attitude of Engagement—The 7 Principles of High Expectations

Let us briefly review our understanding of HEQ so far. We have defined a critical thinking skill. We have learned how critical thinking skills mediate the transition from understanding mere content (facts) to organizing principles, rules, or what we might call concepts. And we have seen that asking questions is particularly effective for helping the student to engage his or her own critical thinking skills.

The next part of learning HEQ is to discover how to create an environment of engagement when using questions as the vehicle for communication between us and our class of students. In my experience, it is unsurprising to say that attitudes are a key factor in learning, perhaps even more than initial cognitive aptitude. If we, as teachers, fail to set the right attitude in our students, even the best questions are unlikely to lead to great learning.

In HEQ, we have a framework for discussing attitudes. We divide them into beliefs or "principles"— 7 of them--and the practices we should do based upon those principles. In HEQ, there are 7 key principles and 7 key practices that govern the expectations or attitudes of the class.

Why is it so important to talk about beliefs in the context of classroom questioning? Beliefs have a strong effect, positively or negatively, upon practice. Even when a particular practice is well known, if the underlying belief system behind it is not firm, people tend to break with the associated practice. For instance, what is that practice we should all follow when we come to a red light? We should stop. But we all know of people who run red lights. Why do they run red lights? Is it because they forgot the practice — to stop at a light that is red — or is it that they no longer believed in the operating principle, that we must obey traffic signs for the safety and convenience of all?

What the red light example should suggest is that often people know what is good practice but choose not to follow it because their belief system isn't strong enough, in moments of stress, to adhere to it. Turning to the context of classroom questioning, it's not enough just to know what the best practices for questioning are; you must engage the area of beliefs and assumptions and notice how they are tied to what we need to do.

Principle 1: We believe that students come to school with the need to learn, and when they are in school, they do not have the right not to learn.

School exists for a reason — to get students to learn the content, concepts and skills required by society. With those skills, they can earn a living, find what inspires them, be independent and even contribute to society as a whole. Sadly, many students do not come to school recognizing their own need to learn. For instance, a common symptom of that lack of recognition would be a failure to do homework. But another sign would be the lack of willingness to answer questions.

Indeed, some students go further and even influence other students not to answer questions. There can be a certain level of group-think in a class, wherein if a few students purposefully try not to answer, even students who would otherwise be willing to answer questions become reluctant to break from the group.

These signals of disengagement are disturbing and blame often gets pointed in an obvious direction. It is true that some parents have simply failed to get their children to take responsibility for the act of being interested in school. How often have you observed a parent suggest that when their student is dropped off at the door, the teacher is responsible for making the student interested in learning? And some administrators acquiesce to this mindset, "Yes, parent, that's right, we'll do even more." I empathize with teachers when I see this, because although there is a grain of truth to it, the fact remains that parents set the stage for the attitude the student brings to school. Is school a place of effort or a place of obstinacy? This is not about who's in charge (which should be the teacher) but about who is putting forth effort (which should be the student).

But parents aren't wholly responsible. Disengaged classroom environments often reflect a common accord between teacher and student, which might be summarized as, "You don't interrupt my class and I won't call on you." I understand there are other factors that contribute to disengagement, from boring content to droning announcements (hate them!), but nothing can be worse for the engagement of the classroom than when teachers and students both agree, "It's okay just to sit there."

Indeed, there is a strong culture in some schools that has developed around the notion that it is okay not to participate if you don't feel like it. For instance, in some classrooms, students are given a "pass" that they can use if they don't want to answer a question. On one hand, the pass can spare a student an embarrassing moment and if it's not overused, it seems okay. On the other hand, in life, people are rarely given passes, "Hello, this is your City Water Department, I'd like to pass." Come to think of it, maybe we do use passes a lot in life! Still, in HEQ, passes are not an option. Passes are a small step, but still a step, towards disengagement.

Another example of how some aspects of the culture of education can reinforce disengagement is the use of "learning styles" as an excuse for non-participation. In workshops, I have heard teachers ask, "But what if he is not an oral learner?" as a reason not to question students. But wait a minute. If a child can speak, the acquisition of language itself suggests that the student is an oral learner. Also, consider whether that student is similarly non-oral in other contexts or even other classrooms? Additionally, many students and even adults misperceive their own learning styles. Have you ever heard a person misdiagnose their personality-type and then you think to yourself, silently, "No way is he the Leadership Type!" Finally, even if students are not "oral-learners," there is a huge price to be paid for that in the future, wherein the ability to communicate orally is likely to be very important. How many opportunities will there be for people who say, "Yeah, I'd love to work here. I just don't like talking to people that much." Keep in mind that there are 300 million people in this country, and most of them talk.

In HEQ, we don't believe all students necessarily want to learn, but with the right prompting and structure, most can learn—begrudgingly, perhaps. So, what do we do based on this firm belief? We call on all the students in the classroom. We may not get to each student in every class period, though, as this is not about counting potatoes. But over a few classes, we want to call on every student.

Not only do we call on all students, we call on them whether or not they volunteer to answer. We call on them with hands up or hands down, smiling or frowning, front of the room or back. As Dr. Lee Hannel says in workshops, "I imagine that I see all students with both hands wildly waving, dying to participate!" Is that actually true for most classrooms? No. But as the teacher, I need to imagine that vision in order to remember to call on everyone in the room.

A practical suggestion is to use checkmarks on a seating chart to make sure you are calling on all students. Everyone has a natural tendency to question to one direction or another, front or back of the room, girls or boys or just certain students. So, the seating chart with checkmarks is a useful tool for making sure you eventually call on all students.

Finally, please remember that calling on all students is a deceptively easy idea but hard to enact in practice. Why would such a simple dictum be hard to enact? Intuitively, as adults we learn to respond to visual or other cues that a person doesn't want to speak to us and respond, often enough, by disengaging.

In workshops, I find the following example helps to explain the natural tendency to disengage the disengaged. Imagine you are alone in an elevator and a person comes onto the lift with you. That person looks at you, briefly makes eye contact, but then stares at his feet, then the elevator buttons, and finally turns his back upon you. What's he saying? He's giving cues that he doesn't want to be engaged. If this were to happen, most of us would leave him alone. Now, instead, imagine that as soon as he turns his back you say to him, "Hello, I have an academic question to ask you." Wouldn't that be difficult? But in a way, that's exactly what HEQ requires us to do, to overcome our own intuitions and still question the elevator-riding student even when they'd prefer to stare at the floor.

Practice: Call on all students whether or not they volunteer.

Principle 2: We believe that students are undertrained, not underbrained; they are dormant, not dead!

In HEQ, we believe that most students, perhaps 90%, bring a physical brain that is capable of acceptable or higher quality performance in academic achievement. We accept that some students have significant cognitive problems due to genetics or accidents, or that some students lead such difficult lives—moving every few months, for example—that it becomes less likely they'll be a part of the 90%. But most students, we believe, can perform acceptably and, more to the point, they should be expected to answer our questions.

In workshops, I have had people say that the 90% standard of HEQ is unrealistic, too high. Given that perhaps 1/3rd or 1/4th of students nationally drop out before or during high school, it does seem that 90% is a very tough standard. Other educators retort that 100% of students should be expected to perform acceptably. I'm stuck between a rock and a hard place! Well, both sides have their points but what I do know is that if 90% of the students in the US were performing acceptably in academic work, we'd all be a lot happier than we are now. So, that's the standard in HEQ.

Believing that 90% of the students in front of you can answer any question you might ask to any other student is hard to do! I've been in workshops where I've looked out on the class and thought, "Whoa, maybe only ½ the students can answer my (grade-level) questions." But each time I've felt that way, I've almost always been surprised how the right questions with the right attitude can lead 90% or an even a higher proportion of students to the desired learning. Basically, if you don't believe in the 90% standard, then you're handicapping yourself and your students right from the start. Still, it often requires a leap of faith to believe that 90% of the students in front of you can answer good, solid questions.

Before we get to the specific classroom practices that are derived from the principle above, let us recognize how, in some schools, the culture of the classroom differs from HEQ. In workshops, educators have openly or privately said of the 90% standard, "Maybe for the Anglo kids..." I can never forget one moment when I was at a charter school in Houston with African-American students and leadership and the principal said, "You know, these kids are from an urban, chaotic place. You can't expect them to answer questions like HEQ! If they were from the suburbs..." The next week, I went to east Texas. The school was African-American in the leadership and student population. What did I hear? "If only the kids had the opportunities you'd find in a big city like Houston..." I've been told that Hispanic kids are culturally different and can't be expected to answer questions, same with Native Americans, or that low socioeconomic students can't answer questions and so on. I'd be rich if I had a dollar for every time someone said, "This group of students can't answer questions." At heart, this mindset seems totally different than what the American spirit is purported to be, adventurous and persevering, as compared to timid and enfeebled.

HEQ requires us to suspend disbelief for a moment and treat students equally. This is not to completely deny cultural differences or factors of engagement that go beyond the classroom. But the thing is, for the 5-30 minutes that a normal HEQ lesson lasts, we can put aside those differences and try to treat students the same.

What are the concrete practices associated with the 90% belief? It means that we must ask students both the same number of questions over time and give them a chance at initial questions with the same level of quality. In HEQ, we talk about the quantity of questions and the quality of questions.

Let's talk about quantity. In terms of quantity, in HEQ we attempt to ask students an equal number of questions over time. That length of time maybe be a week or over the days required to learn a particular concept or however you'd like to structure it. Do not confuse this idea with making sure that each student gets the same number of questions in a single class. In any single class period, some students will have different rates of understanding and may need extra or fewer questions at that precise moment. So, do not get fixated on "2 questions per student per class." It's over a length of time that you affix.

The rationale behind asking an equal number of questions over time is simple. If Student A over a week is asked 30 questions and Student B is asked only 3 questions, I don't care how good those 3 questions are, I think that Student A is going to go farther in learning. Asking about the same number of questions over time helps to produce a classroom in which all students are at least given a similar number of engagement opportunities.

The harder part of the 90% principal is asking questions that are of similar quality—at least initially. Imagine that John is an A student and Mary is a D student. What kind of question would you normally give to John, and what would you give to Mary? Normally, we give the A kind of question to John and the D or maybe C kind of question to Mary. According to HEQ, we have to ask Mary the A or at least B kind of question initially, just as we might for John. It is counterintuitive for most people to ask the "harder" kind of question to the less proficient student.

So, in HEQ, if I feel that the class as a whole should now be prepared to answer questions requiring connection ("Step 2" of HEQ) or application ("Step 6" of HEQ) or some other cognitive act, then I ask questions requiring comparison to any student I see, not just a few. I don't want to "tone it down" for some students from the very start of that step in HEQ.

Perhaps an example will illustrate the opposite practice. I can never forget watching a teacher ask a student a very good question. I can't remember what the teacher asked, but maybe it was something like, "What can you infer from the chapter we just read?" Perhaps she felt that most of the students were prepared to answer questions involving inference. Then, she went on to one particular student and in a lighter and more doubtful voice asked, "Okay, did you read the story? Did you like it?" From her tone as well as the question, I could tell that she perceived this student to be less capable.

Truth be told, the teacher probably was correct in her intuitions about that student's more limited skill. Maybe he was part of the 10%? I don't know. But lowering the level of the question for a student before even asking the kind of question you really want to ask is troubling for at least a few reasons.

The first reason, I believe, is that it does not preserve the dignity of the student to ask them an obviously easier question in the hopes that they will not feel embarrassed in front of their peers. It's not like that student or the other students don't know a soft pitch when they see (or hear) one.

The second and more important reason is that if lower achieving students never hear the harder questions, how will they ever learn to answer them? If it is time to ask a certain kind of question to the class, it's a good idea to ask that kind of question to the 90% who should be ready for it without toning it down, at least at first. If a student fails to respond in the way you had hoped, then you may: reduce the cognitive act of the question; narrow the scope of the content addressed by the question; or just rephrase the question using different language. But again, at least you gave the student a chance at answering it as initially presented.

In HEQ workshops, after the student demo, we often discuss which questions students were able to answer and which ones they had difficulty answering. On occasion, when talking about the ones students were not able to answer, I'll hear a teacher comment, "But he's never heard that kind of question before." Huh? Whose fault is that, then?

We must move away from a "culture of success" where students have to feel good or "successful" about all their responses and to what I call a "culture of effort." It's okay to be wrong as long as you really tried to answer the question. I think the real fear, though, is not from students worried about giving wrong answers than our own fear, as teachers, of hearing poor responses after all our efforts. We so desire to hear forward progress; it's what we want to hear.

Thus, asking the higher quality question at first is hard because it makes us risk the illusion of "success" in the classroom. But successful teaching is not predicated on smooth waters but on strong currents of learning, a mixing of questions and answers, good and bad, and renewed questions. We have to do something counterintuitive and risk failure in our questions in order to hopefully achieve success and learning by students.

A simple way of boiling this down is to try the following. Always think of the question that you, as the teacher, want to ask in a particular "Step" of HEQ (more on this, later). Then, select any student to answer it. Try not to find a student and then think of a tailor-made question for that student. If I have doubts about a student, I don't want to look over at "Ivan" and say, "Hmm, I wonder what I can ask Ivan?" In a split second, I'll probably make the question I was about to ask easier. Rather, I want to think of the question that I'd like to ask anyone in the room, and then ask that question to anyone in the room. I choose my question, and only thereafter do I choose my student.

Practice: Ask students a similar quantity and quality of questions; choose your question and then choose your student.

Principle 3: We believe that intensity makes a difference towards outcomes.

One of the harder parts of HEQ is learning how to ask questions intensively. What does it mean to be intensive? It means that we use questioning as the primary instructional or communication strategy for a defined period of classroom time lasting between 5 to 30 minutes. In HEQ, most of the way in which we communicate with our students is through questions. HEQ requires asking lots and lots of questions.

The HEQ practice of asking mostly questions in a lesson is much easier than it sounds. When students don't give responses that we want to hear, it is easy to go back to telling, showing, hinting, helping, and other non-questioning methods. For example, when a student gives an undesired response to a question, I'll often hear teachers say, "Okay, let me give you a hint." Hinting, however, is not a questioning mode. It's a giving mode.

Of course, you can't be too strict about this. At times, if a student needs a bit of instruction that is best given by a non-questioning means, then do so. If a student asks, "What page are we on?" don't reply with, "What page could we be on?" I've seen this. Be practical but try to stick with questions.

In terms of timeframe, HEQ sessions of 5 to 10 minutes might be appropriate at elementary grades, 10 to

20 minutes for middle grades, while sessions of up to 30+ minutes might be reserved for high school classes. Even though HEQ is intensive, it is not about asking students an uninterrupted series of questions for an hour and a half or anything like that. It's not supposed to be a trial!

In 20 to 30 minutes using HEQ, a teacher might ask students between 50 to 150+ questions. That may seem like a lot of questions, but it happens very quickly. In fact, most students perceive that they have been asked far fewer questions than have actually been queried. Still, for the teacher, HEQ does require asking a lot of questions and that can be tiring. Which is another reason why we tend to limit HEQ sessions to shorter periods of time.

Compare the intensity of HEQ questioning to classrooms in which questions are being asked but in a different way. Often, in non-HEQ settings, teachers do ask questions but they may ask far fewer questions overall and spread them out over the course of an entire lesson. The non-HEQ setting may see 20 questions asked over the course of fifty minutes. While it is conceivable that asking fewer questions in total might lead students to the same learning objective, it is less likely and also reduces the potential number of respondents. If there are twenty-five students in a room and we ask 100 questions, we can assume that most students will receive about 4 questions. If only 10 questions are asked in that same time period, most students will never be questioned.

Why is intensity in questioning so important? Intensity via questioning forces the brain to be more active than when questions are asked with a lesser frequency. Look at the physical domain, where intensity seems to make a difference to outcomes. If two athletes are put into the same pool for an hour's practice, one an Olympic swimmer and the other an average swimmer, what is the difference in the way they train? HEQ demands mental, rather than physical intensity from the student.

When asking all these questions, it is important that most students participate. But we also don't want to follow a rule of "one question per student" and then move on to another student. Many teachers follow a pattern of one question per student without even realizing it. They try to keep the class moving, so to speak, and feel that if they spend more than one or two questions in a row with a single student, that it risks other students becoming inattentive. In HEQ, you may ask an individual student between 1 to 3 consecutive questions or even a few more with discretion.

Why does HEQ require that we create not just an overall intensity in questioning of the class but also brief moments in which an individual student may be asked several questions in a row? One reason is that some students may not be at the cusp of a learning moment and require an initial question, a follow-up question, and maybe even another follow-up question to reach a new understanding. The student is not going to cross a cognitive threshold unless he receives a follow-up question and maybe another question after that. If we don't allow ourselves to ask an individual student more than one question, then we might be spreading the questions too thinly.

Another reason for allowing ourselves to ask a few consecutive questions to an individual student is that it benefits the listening habits of peers. Occasionally, in workshops, I'll hear someone say, "But when you were asking X that follow-up question, I noticed Y was tuning out." Well, what should be done instead, ask Y questions and discover that X is tuning out?

The underlying problem here is that some students have not learned how to listen when other students are speaking. They do not make a habit of listening. How often do non-answering students carefully listen to what another student is saying or responding for, say, thirty seconds? But if we don't condition our students to listening, because we are afraid they will tune out while another student is speaking, then we'll never get anywhere. If our students can't listen for thirty seconds in a row, that seems to me to be a big problem.

The ideal situation, of course, is to pepper the room so that most students participate but at least some get a chance to answer a few questions in a row. There must be a balance between the needs of the responding student and the needs of the other, non-responding students to participate and the desire to move forward in the lesson itself.

Finally, the most important reason for asking questions intensively is that it actually reduces the level of anxiety in the classroom about asking and answering questions. Think for a moment: What would be less intimidating, a class where 10 questions are asked over the period or 100 questions? Most people would think that the class of fewer questions is less intimidating. How could it be that asking more and more questions leads to reduced student anxiety? Wouldn't one expect the opposite?

Consider it like this: Imagine that you are a student in a class and the teacher usually asks very few questions in any period. A lot is riding on each question. Then, when you are asked a question and don't respond in the intended way, how would you feel? Compare this to a class period in which a hundred questions are asked. When you miss one of them, well, it's not as big a deal. Less is riding on each question.

With so many questions being asked and answered, there will be other students who also have missed a question. And with all those extra questions being asked, you might very well have a chance to answer a question correctly and overcome the prior instance of a less-than-stellar response. Thus, asking more questions leads to a more positive and risk-taking learning environment than when very few questions are asked.

That intensive questioning leads to more students asking questions should make sense to you by now. It is a form of modeling behavior. If students see lots of questioning by the teacher, they will likely model that type of learning style on their own. If few questions are asked, they will also get that message, "Don't interrupt me with a question." For the same reason that we behave in church but become rowdy in a baseball stadium, a classroom of few questions reinforces student passivity. So, keep in the questioning mode during HEQ!

Practice: Ask mostly questions and refrain from telling, hinting, helping or other non-questioning modes.

Principle 4: We believe that the justification is as important as the answer given.

Many students have learned to give answers without thinking in response to questions. If you've ever heard students simply repeat a nearby student's answer, you'll know what I'm talking about. Simply giving a response does not attend to having any mental intensity behind it. The student's response must have reasoning—their own--to be valuable to learning.

"Is it...42?"
"Is it...Guatamala?"

Students have learned to condition us, as teachers, to a low level of expectation about the reasoning that supports their responses. They can even get us to give them the answers to the very questions we ask! For instance, have you ever heard a student complete a response with a question mark at the end? The student will give an answer, but instead of saying, "42" or "Bolivia" they'll say, "Is it...42???" or "Boliiiivvviaaa?"

In workshops, I'll ask teachers what they think a student is really trying to say by responding with a question mark at the end. Often, I'll hear that the student must simply not be sure of his or her answer. But I think it's more than that. Otherwise, why don't students say something like, "Well, I think the probability of my answer is low, but I'm going to stick with 42 as my answer." No, students rarely do this. The answer with a question mark is more than "I'm not sure," it's also "And you tell me what I should say next." It's more like when you ask your spouse where the remote is and they say, "In the kitchen???" It's more than "I'm not sure," it's really "Go to the kitchen and find it yourself." When this happens in the classroom, teachers often jump in and begin to help students rather than continuing in a questioning mode.

I always think of a particular situation I experienced to remind me of why answering with a question mark can be problematic in life. Years ago, I had asked a subcontractor to bid on remodeling two old bathrooms. I waited as he inspected them and reviewed his notes in front of me. Finally, I asked him for an approximate bid. He replied with, "Uh, well, how about $5,000?" I remained silent as I thought about the bid, and in a moment he replied, "What about $4,000?" I decided to see what might happen and just stayed quiet. "$3,250?" I began to sense that he really didn't know what he expected from the job in terms of money, which made wonder about the job itself. I gave the work to someone who had a higher bid but could explain to me the reasons for the price requested.

In order to get students to have reasoning to support their responses, HEQ requires that we follow a certain pattern in our oral questioning called question-response-question (Q-R-Q). For instance, I may ask Nick an initial question. Then, Nick responds. Regardless of whether Nick's answer is right or wrong, I always ask him to justify his initial response. A question, then a response, then a follow-up question.

You don't always have to ask the follow-up question to the student who gave the initial response. If I ask Nick a question and he gives a response, I may ask Maria to try to justify Nick's initial response. As the teacher, you don't want to be too predictable and always call on the student who initially responds to give the justification. If you do that, other students will notice the pattern and know they won't be asked the next question, so they'll take what I call a micro-nap. If you've ever been riding in a car and suddenly realized you were starring off into space, you'll know what a micro-nap is.

Although it should go without saying, use your judgment about when to ask the follow-up question for justification. If you ask a student, "What color is that circle?" and she responds, "Blue," you probably don't need to ask, "And how do you know it's blue?" I've seen this.

Again, remember to ask the follow-up question whether the student's initial response is right or wrong, excellent or mediocre in quality. Be sure to ask students to justify both answers that are exactly what you had hoped to hear and those that fall short. Just say, "How can you justify that answer?" or "Where is evidence for that in the text?" or "How do you know that?

Lastly, many teachers have been taught to reflexively "validate" all answers given by students, even those responses given without reasoning. This is actually a misrepresentation of how the word validate is defined according to The American Heritage Dictionary, which is "to establish the soundness of; corroborate." In HEQ, we do not "praise" answers given without reasoning. I'd rather hear a wrong answer with strong reasoning behind it than the best answer with no reasoning to support it. So, encourage answers that have reasoning behind them but do not praise answers given with no thought or reasoning to them, unless you want to encourage that same lack of thought in the future.

Practice: Ask students to justify answers.

Principle 5: We believe in keeping our environment positive but pushy.

Questioning can take a negative turn without the teacher even knowing it. In HEQ, we believe in keeping the questioning environment positive overall. This means we remain aware of the tone of our questions and avoid questions whose inquiry is negative.

When we say that some questions have a "negative inquiry," we are describing questions like:

- Weren't you listening?'
- Did you even read the question?
- Is that your final answer?
- Is that really an eighth grade sort of answer?
- Why don't you know that?

Even if one were to phrase these kinds of questions a bit more diplomatically, like, "Do you have an undiagnosed cognitive problem that we don't know about?" these negative-inquiry questions still are not a good idea.

My favorite negative question, if one can have such a thing, was when I observed a teacher ask a student, "But if you did know the answer, what would it be?" Huh? Interestingly, I have had teachers swear that this kind of question works, but I still think it's negative and avoid it. It reminds me too much of the, "If a tree fell in the forest" kind of question.

Anyway, these kinds of questions do not have a good answer and, no matter their tone, almost always create a negative environment. Notice these are mostly rhetorical questions. The student isn't really expected to answer them. But most questions that are negative become that way because of their tone. Compare asking a student, "How did you get that?" with "How did you get THAT?" The questions are the same in structure or inquiry but very different in the asking.

While HEQ requires we avoid negativity in our questions, this does not mean that we can avoid being demanding or become passive in our questioning. Sometimes, when we ask questions to students that are trying hard not to answer, it's frustrating to stay perfectly neutral or positive. In fact, keeping a totally happy face when students are purposefully not putting effort forth seems strange to both teachers and students. So, we say to be realistic and realize that the best approach is to be "pushy but positive."

In workshops during the student demonstration, a teacher might notice that out of 150 questions asked, perhaps a few did not come out in a perfectly positive way or that a student did not like it when asked a certain question. Don't confuse the forest with the trees, as the saying goes. A few negative questions probably won't turn into a negative environment if the majority of questions are positive. So be pushy but stay positive!

Practice: Ask questions with a neutral to positive tone and avoid rhetorical questions.

Principle 6: We believe in purposeful rather than random inquiry.

When asked questions, many students like to simply guess at answers. It has become part of the culture of the classroom, perhaps due to the prominence of multiple-choice exams. While we cannot prevent students from giving us guesses, we should not encourage them to guess. That is, we don't want students to simply pick or give answers at random. Indeed, one of the reasons we enact the Q-R-Q pattern from Principle 4 is to reduce guess-making behavior.

Without evening knowing it, teachers may be asking students to guess without thinking. Consider how the following common questions encourage a guess-making approach:

- Can you take a guess?
- Can you take an educated guess?
- Can you try, again?
- I know you chose C, but could it be D?

The culture of some classrooms also encourages guess-making behavior by students. Some educators feel that participation is paramount, whether or not there is actual thinking going on. I was once asked by a principal to visit a classroom in a school in California. From a position behind the door, I could see most students raising their hands to answer. The principal commented, "Isn't this a great, risk-taking learning environment?"

I opened the door slightly to better hear the questions and responses by students. Many of the responses given by students were just guesses. There was nothing behind them. The teacher would accept a guess and then solicit yet another guess and then yet another guess. While the environment had much participation, most of it was predicated upon student non-thought. This random inquiry environment is not HEQ. It is generating a lot of heat but probably little light.

You can also see other patterns of questioning that encourage guess-making behavior. For instance, as a test-taking strategy, students are sometimes told to "look at the test questions, then look at the content." Is that how we should encourage comprehension of material for the long-term? Another test-taking strategy that seems more akin to guessing is a simple associative pattern like this, "If you see the word 'opinion' in the question, look for the answer that has 'believe' in it." The student may not know why the answer is actually an opinion but relies mostly on a guess-making pattern to select an answer-choice.

In HEQ, we want to teach students to think before they respond. We try to avoid questions that seem like they might encourage random answers. If we hear a lot of random answers, that's a signal, our questioning is going astray in some way.

In workshops, some teachers ask whether precluding guessing also precludes the act of asking for predictions? The answer is clearly no. When we ask someone for a "prediction," we are asking for something entirely different than a "guess." And while some predictions may be probabilistic, not all guesses involve the act of prediction. Some guesses are just that, guesses without thinking.

Practice: Don't ask for guesses.

Principle 7: We believe that "I don't know" is mostly a learned behavior to avoid engagement.

One of the most common responses that students can give to questions is to reflexively answer, "I don't know." Some students may say, "I don't have to" or simply shrug their shoulders or stare into space. If we, as teachers, cannot reliably overcome the "I don't know" kind of response, our questioning will become ineffective. When students see that "I don't know" effectively removes them from participating, other students often imitate that behavior so as to avoid engagement.

In HEQ, whenever a student answers with "I don't know" and the teacher thinks that this reflects a desire to avoid participating, we immediately follow-up with 1 to 3 additional questions to the same student. By asking additional questions immediately after the student says, "I don't know," we teach them that "I don't know" is likely to lead to more engagement, not less. We usually don't go beyond asking 3 or 4 consecutive questions to a student, though.

In workshops, I am often asked, what if a student remains quiet throughout a series of questions? What can be done? HEQ does not offer an immediate cure for the disengaged student who decides to avoid all participation. We might also recognize that this same disengagement probably is occurring during other forms of instruction, such as lecture, only that the questions make it obvious—they unmask the disengaged student. The best we can do is simply return to the student at a later time and again attempt to ask him a few questions. And what if the student really, truly doesn't know? At least the additional questions might bring about some degree of understanding. They also tell the student that it is important to try to know.

The reason "I don't know" responses are so detrimental is, though it may be accepted in school, American culture, as a whole does not agree with people who don't know or don't seem like they are trying to know. Two quick stories may help to illustrate this.

I was once at a Wal-Mart and watched as a customer found an assistant manager in the aisle and asked him where she could find a certain item. The manager said that being new to the particular store, he didn't have an exact idea where the item was. He didn't know. The customer become angry and felt that the manager should have known. Did it ever occur to the customer that it might be unfair to expect someone to know where one of several thousand items in a huge store might be? No, because knowing was the expectation. I left before the situation was resolved but imagine all the fuss was over Spam or something like that.

Another time, I was waiting in the Houston airport for my delayed connecting flight on Southwest Airlines. The originating flight from Dallas was supposed to carry me to San Antonio, then El Paso, and then Phoenix. You don't have a lot of patience for delays in that sort of trip. When a delay of two hours was announced, I asked a gate attendant, "When exactly is the plane coming in?" in fear of becoming stranded at one of the airports en route. The attendant replied, "I don't know."

But that's not all he did. He also said, "Let me call Dallas and see when the plane left. And, if it's too late in arrival, let me see if we can get you to another airline that gets into Phoenix. Just wait here at the gate for a few minutes, I'll make you comfortable, and we'll find out where to go."

Contrast this attitude with that of some students. I've never heard a student say, after an "I don't know response," something like, "I don't know now, but let me search the Internet for that information, go back into the textbook, and if you wait here for fifteen minutes, I'll have an answer for you." In short, many students don't feel an urgent need to know. HEQ encourages students to try to know.

Practice: Ask 1 to 3 more questions after an "I don't know" response.

CHAPTER SIX:

IMPORTANT THEORIES
ABOUT QUESTIONING

In previous chapters, we considered how attitudes, expectations and phrasing impact the use of questioning in the classroom. Now, we'll switch gears and discuss some of the ideas or concepts that are often referred to when thinking about classroom questioning. Many readers will be somewhat familiar with these constructs, which include:

- Question-stems
- Essential questions
- Bloom's Taxonomy

   I will also add a concept that we use in HEQ called the Cognitive Structure of Information to this list.

   Let's start with the simplest concepts about questioning and go from there. The ideas do get complicated, though, so be sure not to get too wrapped or worried about a complete understanding upon first reading. Let the ideas sit in your head for a while.

Question Stems

Many schools and districts have tried to hurry-up the process of asking higher order questions by simply giving teachers lists of verb stems to use in their oral and written classroom questioning. You'll see those verbs provided like this: "to compare" or "to analyze" or "to predict." Yes, HEQ uses similar verbs. Given the nature of English, there are only so many verbs to use altogether. There is nothing wrong with the verbs at all.

   But the problem with providing simple verb lists, as with providing teachers with the levels of Bloom's Taxonomy, is that just memorizing a list of verbs is about as likely to encourage good classroom questioning as memorizing the multiplication table is likely to result in good mathematical understanding. It's a first step, but if you don't know how and why you are trying to solve a particular problem, the fact that you have 6 x 8 memorized as "48" doesn't help much. In a way, those verb lists make me think that teachers are perceived as so lacking in understanding, that we are just given lists of verbs in the hope we'll use them. I feel like saying, "I've never seen these remarkable words before! Thank you!"

   The real problem is that without an understanding of the cognitive acts behind those verb stems—why don't students "identify" correctly—then all those lists of verbs are likely to be left unasked. As you'll learn, HEQ provides a comprehensive understanding behind "why" we're asking certain kinds of questions, not just the verbs logically associated with them.

Essential Questioning

Another concept that is often related to questioning strategies is asking students "essential questions" by Robert Marzano.

   I can't do justice to the entire concept of essential questions in this space alone. But some of the elements of what makes a question essential include that it:

(a) goes to the heart of a discipline
(b) has no one obvious "right" answer
(c) uses higher-order questions according to Bloom's taxonomy
(d) recurs throughout one's learning
(e) provokes student interest
(f) links to other questions

   There is nothing wrong with asking essential questions. However, asking students meaningful, complicated questions requires a confidence that students' basic cognitive skills, as required by the content area, have been developed and are independently active. Asking a question like, "What should be the next kind of vehicle engine design, and synthesize the benefits and drawbacks as compared to the current internal combustion motor?" would probably trigger a great deal of thinking and interest in a budding automotive engineer. Asking the same question to a person who has never opened the hood of a car might not be so immediately profitable to learning.

This is not to say that essential questions should not be asked. Like any framework for questioning or thinking, if it works, then use it. But in my experience, the legions of underachieving students that I regularly see in classrooms have not been able to profit from essential questions, perhaps due to the underdevelopment of a cohort of substantive cognitive skills. It also occurs to me that some textbooks construct their chapter-review questions in a manner akin to essential questions. I cannot say whether those written essential questions have benefited the average student or not.

I think the reason essential questions are popular is due less to their success in changing the low or average student's thinking than in the fact that they spark interest amongst adult teachers. Essential questions are very interesting and exciting! Who wouldn't want to discuss interesting, important questions? But the difference between the cognition of adults and students expresses the need for school itself. Overcoming that cognitive abyss, according to HEQ, often requires many smaller and more tactical questions rather than larger, more complicated ones. Could essential questions trigger or generate the many smaller questions needed for understanding? It is conceivable. Use your own judgment as to whether your students or subject matter would benefit from asking essential questions, following HEQ's framework for questioning or a combination of the two.

Bloom's Taxonomy

Bloom's Taxonomy is often linked to questioning. In the 1950s, Benjamin Bloom created a framework for categorizing the level of abstraction of the mental acts that students need to develop. Many teachers have been exposed to Bloom's Taxonomy at a superficial level in workshops or college. Given teachers' common general knowledge of Bloom's Taxonomy, I have often wondered why so few teachers seem to be able to implement it in their questioning of students.

I do not have a compelling reason why Bloom's Taxonomy (or even the revised Taxonomy by Anderson and Krathwohl) has not resonated with educators except at a cursory level. I suspect the reason is less unfamiliarity with the "levels" of Bloom's as the inability to articulate why the levels are structured in the way that they are. Through HEQ, I hope that you will learn the reasons why, in terms of cognition, we organize our questions into particular levels or, more accurately, steps of thinking and how those steps are similar and different than Bloom's Taxonomy.

The Cognitive Scaffold

The "cognitive scaffold" is a common conceptual metaphor of how to structure or organize questions for effective learning. While the metaphor is frequently used, I do not think that many people have explored it very deeply. So, let's take a look!

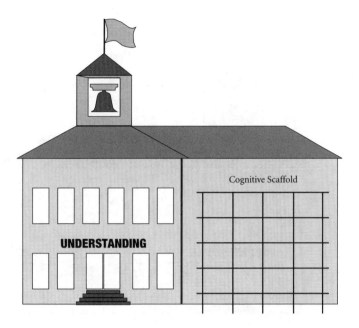

I find it helpful to visualize an actual scaffold climbing a building as a first step in understanding. You may think of each rung of the scaffold as representing questions that go higher and higher in terms of the critical thinking skills to be elicited.

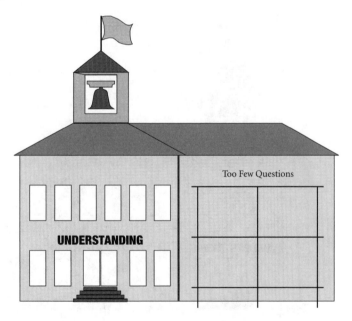

Notice that to climb the scaffold our questions must be organized in a way to develop lower to higher order thinking skills. But consider what happens when there are too few rungs (or questions) being asked as the construction worker (student) tries to climb the scaffold. If there are too few rungs, metaphorically, "holes" are left in the scaffold. The student may not be able to reach for the next level of thinking; he cannot make the (mental) stretch for the next rung. If, in our oral questioning, we skip asking certain kinds of questions or ask too few of them—if we lower the intensity of questioning--we space the rungs out and make things much harder for the student to climb.

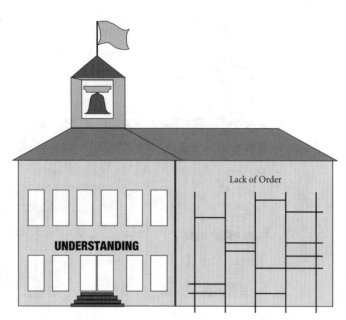

Imagine, instead, there are sufficient rungs (questions) but they are randomly placed. That is, questions are asked but without any attention to order. It is very hard to move upwards a scaffold that way. Most of the (mental) movement remains from side to side or even downward.

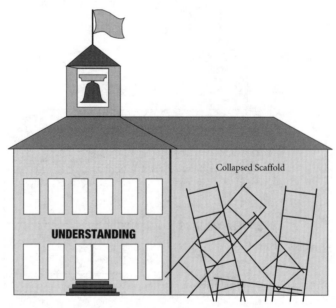

According to the cognitive scaffold, when the intensity and order of our questions are not accounted for, a significant problem may ensue. In terms of questioning, when the cognitive scaffold has too many holes, not only does the individual worker get stuck somewhere therein, but also the entire scaffold (of understanding/information) can collapse! That is to say, the entire information matrix becomes so weak that nothing can be done from a position within the scaffold; one has to go back to the very beginnings to re-construct the scaffold from the foundations.

This "collapsing scaffold" resonates with how often students can seem to "miss" entire sections of information. Students, and thus teachers, go back to the beginnings because the cognitive scaffold has collapsed entirely. Thus, the metaphor of the cognitive scaffold fundamentally teaches us about the need for order and intensity in the elicitation of mental acts. Even the phrase "higher order thinking skills" has the word "order" in it, probably for a reason. There is a cognitive order to good questioning. And if we, as teachers, cannot articulate that order and why it is the way it is, our questioning is very likely to proceed in random ways.

The need for order in questioning should also resonate with our own experience, which informs us that ordered questioning leads to learning but randomly asked questions rarely do. Can we observe a situation in which good questions are being asked but in a random way? In fact, we can.

Many of our state exit exams are comprised entirely of questions, usually 50-120 of them per exam or something like that. That's a lot of questions. Also, the questions range in difficulty from those that are considered to be "easy" and require lower order thinking and those that are "hard" and require more thinking. A reasonable observer might ask, "If asking questions is so good, and harder or higher-level questions are even better, then why don't students seem to benefit from taking state exams in terms of learning?" Indeed, I have never heard a student say, "Wow, thanks for letting me take that state exam! This whole past year of sitting in your classroom was okay, but that state exam really brought it all together for me, made me understand!"

Why don't the questions on state exams or most written exams lead to learning? One reason may be that there is no cognitive order to the written questions on exams. Of course, the purpose of such exams is not to teach but to assess. Still, the point holds that ordering of questions is key to understanding. As a side note, notice there is also no Q-R-Q process to be enacted when students take an exam (that would be cheating). But when it comes to oral classroom questioning, HEQ acknowledges the need for order in questioning--and Q-R-Q, for that matter.

A common misunderstanding made by some educators who are unaware of the implications of the cognitive scaffold is to suggest that teachers solely concentrate on asking "higher order questions." When I hear this, I quietly think to myself, one cannot simply wish the students away to the top of the cognitive mountain (it would be nice, but…)! Like any mountain, the cognitive order of operations must be developed or climbed in some sort of order from low to high. Often, students who have problems in answering higher order questions also exhibit failure in some lower levels. Thus, developing the range of cognitive acts in order is one of the strong inferences that may be made from the cognitive scaffold.

Stepping-Stones Across a River

In recognition of the cognitive scaffold, it is often inferred that the kinds of questions used to develop higher order thinking skills will always be necessarily more difficult for students to answer than the questions used to develop lower order thinking skills.

From experience, I can say that for some students, the hardest questions to answer are not always at the top of our scaffold. How can it be that the student might find the higher order questions easier to answer than the lower order questions (once those lower order questions have themselves been answered)? Why might it actually be easier for the teacher to ask the higher order questions than the lower order questions?

This situation actually makes much sense. Consider the following example. Many students can apply—a higher order skill—the Pythagorean theorem quite well after they understand it in general. They can properly "apply" $a^2 + b^2 = c^2$. They can find out what c^2 is if given a^2 and b^2 in a simple application of the theorem.

On the other hand, may come connections expressed in that algorithm, or inferable from it, can be more difficult for students to ascertain, such as that $b^2 = c^2 - a^2$ or $b = \sqrt{(c^2 - a^2)}$. The acts of inference required to see or know these more subtle relationships or derivations can be harder than actually "applying" $a^2 + b^2 = c^2$ in a specific context.

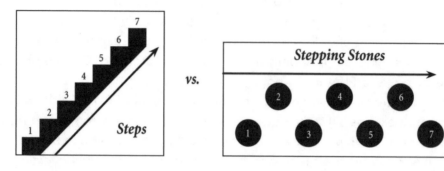

To express this situation in which the difficulty of questions is not always progressively harder, we can use a new metaphor. We can use the metaphor of stepping-stones across a river rather than a scaffold climbing upwards. In this metaphor, the student must still attempt to cross a river (of content) by leaping sequentially from stone to stone (or cognitive act to cognitive act). But the slipperiest stone is not always amongst those near the other side of the river. A student may encounter more difficulty with the mental leaps required to go across the first few stones rather than the law few stones.

The stepping-stones metaphor is useful for several reasons. First, it reinforces the idea that our questions must be sequential in cognitive development. Second, it reminds us that we must use our questions to get students all the way across the "cognitive river" lest they remain stuck in midstream; we must try to get to the farthest kinds of mental acts. Third, students may experience the difficulty of each step of questioning in a way that is not always linear or progressively harder. For some students, the most difficult questions to answer may be at the beginning or middle of a lesson, not at the end.

Cognitive Structure of Information

As you will soon read, successful questioning requires that we ask questions according to a particular cognitive order. In HEQ, we recognize that the mind approaches information in a sequence. But in addition to recognizing how the mind approaches information, we also must recognize how information presents itself to our students and us. Let us explore both of these ideas.

According to HEQ, the average person looks at information in a particular series of steps. HEQ does not pretend to describe the actual mechanisms of the brain at the levels of neurons, as it is true that the mind operates very quickly and may process information in parallel. HEQ only says that for the purposes of teaching, we can organize the mental acts that students should do as they approach information into a particular series of steps, which we trigger through questions.

In order to understand how a person looks at new information, we approach a new concept or body of content by asking ourselves, "How would the student see (or understand) this information if she or he had never seen it before?" This is actually a very difficult question to ask, because it requires trying to imagine that we are back in a first position of understanding. We have to imagine we don't know something.

When you are "the teacher" of that information, it requires a lot of imagination to go back to the beginnings. People try to make this sound easy to do. Have you ever heard the saying, "Forget your assumptions?" A good reply to that might be, "Easier said than done." It's hard to forget our assumptions because we often don't know what assumptions we actually hold! We are not aware of them. What HEQ asks us to do is not to forget our assumptions but to open our eyes and imagine you are seeing something for the first time. What would you notice, see, understand? That's also hard to do!

The second idea that HEQ asks us to keep in mind goes beyond approaching things from the perspective of the (unknowing) student or learner. It also asks we consider how the information on the page or diagram or content wants itself to be understood. You might be thinking, "But how can a page want itself to be understood? It doesn't appear to want anything!"

Well, consider for a moment that all our textbooks, worksheets, videos, diagrams and so on are really just the previous expressions of cognition or thinking done by people before us. The written page is someone else's thinking plus time collapsed into paper. You might say that embedded within even a worksheet is a way of understanding that the "author" is trying to communicate to us.

It can be mentally taxing to look at a sheet of paper, say from a math textbook, and ask, "What does the page intend to show us?" But notice how the page proceeds from top to bottom. Notice if something is numbered. Notice how the titles and subtitles are organized, or where a photo or a diagram is placed. Obviously, information that is pure text, like from a novel, will not have such obvious cues. But it is still possible to see a page or chapter as its own presentation or expression of thought. The content obviously says something, but the way the content is organized also says something to us.

I call this way of looking at the cognition of the student and the embedded cognition of the content as the "cognitive structure of information." The two key questions to ask yourself before mapping out your own classroom questions are: "How does the learner see the information?" and "How does the information want to be seen?" Then, from there, we can attend to the specific cognitive acts that lead to understanding, which we'll address in the next chapter. When we ask these two fundamental questions to ourselves, we as teachers often ask our students much better questions.

CHAPTER SEVEN:

THE BASIC BUILDING BLOCK:
THE COGNITIVE ACT

It's time to learn about the core of HEQ. Before we do that, I want to take a moment to put into perspective the information you are about to read. I do not see or envision HEQ as a complete pedagogy or methodology of teaching. I do not label or describe it as such because pedagogies must have a consistency in their application that is not required by HEQ. Instead, I see HEQ more as a description of how questioning can impact learning. From these descriptions, we as teachers can decide how to approach the questioning process in our own ways.

Consider this as a metaphor. A "diet" requires that a person follow a consistent regimen of eating according to particular rules. When all the rules that describe the diet are not followed with diligence, most people would say that the dieter is not truly following the diet. But HEQ is not like a diet—or in education language, a "program"--with a set of rules that you must follow, all of them, in a particular way.

Instead, HEQ offers descriptions of ideas about oral questioning and how questions, through certain patterns, can improve learning. But HEQ does not stipulate that you must ask your questions in an attempt to adhere strictly to it. HEQ is more akin to a description of healthy eating habits, perhaps a "food pyramid" of cognition, than a particular diet of questions you must follow exactly.

One clear implication of this is that you, as a teacher, are afforded significant flexibility in your questioning habits. If the description HEQ provides of the "cognitive scaffold" or a particular kind of questioning makes sense to you, then use it. If you need to modify a suggestion, then do so. If you can use some but not all of the ideas of HEQ, that's fine. HEQ does not envision the teacher as a mechanical instrument for asking questions; the teacher in HEQ must also think critically and discover how questioning works best in his or her classroom environment.

Cognitive Acts

Learning to ask questions effectively begins with understanding the cognitive acts that underlie questions. In HEQ, each question is a "trigger" for a certain kind of thinking. We use common verbs like asking students to "label" or "compare" or "predict" and focus our attention on the verb, more accurately, the underlying mental act that a question will elicit. Simply put, we ask questions to initiate the student's mind to think in certain ways.

We try to make the language used in our questions seem natural. For instance, one HEQ verb is "to sequence," but we might just as easily ask the student to "put things in order" or to "organize by date" or something like that which is consistent with "sequencing." While HEQ encourages natural language to make students feel comfortable, it's important to balance this with using the more academic or formal language of school. Go ahead and use verbs like compare, predict, infer and so on.

On more than a few occasions, I have heard teachers explain an older student's lack of understanding of a written question as, "He's never heard or seen that word [verb] before." I often ask myself how this is possible? How can a student not be familiar with certain verbs common to tests and so on after years of school?

Maybe we are toning it down too much for students at times? Remember, the language on written exam questions generally uses more academic verbiage and it is important that students become comfortable with those words, too. So, sometimes, rather than saying, "How are these two people the same?" it is important that you ask, "How might these two people be compared?" In HEQ, we balance between natural and formal language in our articulation of questions.

HEQ groups the different kinds of thinking into seven categories. Roughly speaking, the verbs of

Step 1—to label, find, see and notice—are similar in cognitive act. The same is true for the other steps. Because the categories are to be enacted in a sequential order, we call them "steps" of thinking.

This point is important, that the steps are sequential in nature. Otherwise, we might simply call the core of HEQ something like, "7 Different Kinds of Thinking" rather than "7 Steps to Critical Thinking." We'll refer to these as the "7 Steps" from now on. If you might remember from previous chapters, without order our questions become like the random questions on a test that pay little attention to the cognitive development of content.

Cognitive Insight

Now, we may move towards examining each of the 7 Steps. But before we do so, there are a few ideas that are important to touch upon. The first idea is that when we ask students a question in a particular step and they have trouble answering it, this gives us a window into the mind of the student. For instance, if I ask a student to make an inference and the student is unable to do so, this is an obvious signal that the student may need additional questions based on the mental act of inference. This is not an exact science of course. But knowing where a student fails cognitively gives us a way of understanding their lack of understanding.

Too often, when students are not able to answer questions properly, I'll hear teachers explain that lack of success in ways that really don't help to diagnose the actual problem. Consider some of the following statements and you'll see what I mean:

- "He just doesn't get it."
- "They keep forgetting this."
- "Seems like he's missing something."
- "Something's just not clicking."
- "I don't know why she doesn't understand."
- "Brain dead."

Okay, nobody has ever said, "brain dead" but I thought I'd add that in there. At least when we have a framework of cognitive acts, we can say that the student isn't "making connections" or "identifying information" or has problems in "summarizing segments of information." In short, it gives us as teachers a way to communicate about student learning to ourselves, students, and other teachers. The language of cognitive acts becomes a language of understanding about understanding.

Speaking in terms of cognitive acts via the 7 Steps also helps in another way. There are certain common concepts that we want students to understand throughout school, such as "main idea" or "theme" or "algorithm." But when a student misperceives the main idea of a passage, I'll often hear something like, "He doesn't understand the concept of main idea." As above, simply saying the student doesn't get the "main idea" doesn't tell us WHY he doesn't understand the main idea. This kind of reasoning turns the concept of the main idea into an irreducible thing that you either understand or don't.

But if we shift gears and learn to think of a main idea as something developed via a sequence of mental acts—labeling, connection, ordering and summarization—then we can better identify in which area of cognition the student is having trouble. Perhaps the student can label but can't make connections or can do both of those but has trouble establishing the order of events in a story. That sort of knowledge gives us a way of focusing our questions on the specific cognitive acts that hinder the student from understanding the main idea of something.

Cognitive Failure Is Common

An understanding of cognitive acts will help us to diagnose where students falter in understanding. But we must go even deeper. We must ask ourselves, why do students have trouble in the seven kinds of cognitive acts described by the 7 Steps? For instance, we'll soon examine Step 1, which involves identifying, finding, or labeling the key facts in a selection of content. Why don't students identify properly? There must be reasons behind cognitive failure beyond simply saying, "He doesn't identify key facts well." Okay, but why?

It turns out that perfect cognition is perfectly uncommon. When we look at each of the 7 Steps, we'll try to understand why students are likely to have problems in cognition at each step. With that realization, we'll be able to approach our questioning with a sense of purpose. Our role is to correct and guide cognition to the desired outcomes moment by moment (step by step) via questioning.

CHAPTER EIGHT:

STEP ONE

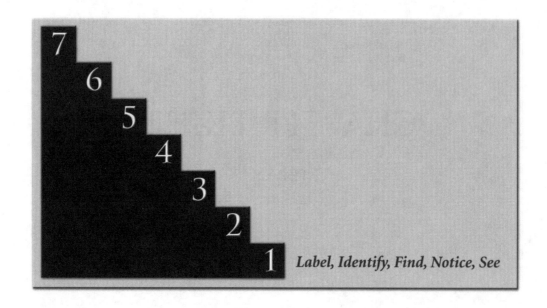

Step 1

The very first kind of mental act of critical thinking that we ask students to do is to label, identify or find the key information in a given selection of content. I often begin a lesson by asking students, "What do you see?" on the page or "What are the key facts?" in the paragraph. If the lesson encompasses several or even tens of pages of information, I might ask, "What are key facts from the unit or chapter?"

Some educators rightly note that this first step of labeling is a lower order thinking skill. This is of course correct. But without this skill, students will be unable to answer higher order questions. If you don't know the key facts, how can inferences or summarizations or predictions be made accurately or made at all?

Random Labeling

One of the cognitive problems I notice during even this first step of critical thinking is that many students can label but they label randomly. For example, they will look at a graph but seem to look at it from the inside and then go out. They'll fail to notice the legend or the horizontal axis but delve deeply into some random point of data. When reading text, students will often tell me about the first or last sentence rather than telling me about the key sentences or paragraphs.

This situation of students labeling but doing so without much attention to the relevancy of information should puzzle us as teachers. I believe that most teachers during lecture or modeling properly illustrate the facts of a lesson in the order in which it should be understood (well, usually). Assuming that we have taught students how to "look at" a graph or "read" a story, why do many underachieving students seem to label, identify, or find information—basic skills--in seemingly random ways?

Natural Differences in Perception

One way of understanding why students may label in seemingly random ways is to note the role of perception and recognize how our perceptions often differ. Simply put, people often naturally see or observe things differently. Consider a car accident. If you have ever heard two accounts of a car accident, you'll know that they sometimes don't match up at all. Or think of a foul in a basketball game. Does everyone call the foul the same way? Our perceptions become very different even due to minor differences in initial position, timing, previous understanding, and so forth. If we can remember the idea that even in very basic or concrete situations, we often notice things differently that we assume should be seen or understood the same, then we can better approach how to question students in the "simple" act of labeling during the abstract work of school.

Absence of Feedback Mechanisms

The explanation that we simply see things in different ways resonates with our common intuitions and offers us one insight into why labeling—a lower level critical thinking skill—can be difficult to properly enact. There is also a second explanation as to why students may label without attention to the underlying relevancy of information.

Most of us as adults unknowingly hold a belief that the feedback mechanisms of the physical world carry over into the world of the classroom. In the physical world of experience, we often learn the underlying relevancy of information through feedback from the environment. Consider two examples.

Have you ever nearly merged into a car next to you while driving (or vice versa)? If this has ever happened to you, did you think to yourself just before impact, "That's a terrific paint job on that car?" If you did, stay off the roads! Why didn't you notice the color of the vehicle and focused instead on its size or proximity? Experience has taught you that a car's color is not very important in avoiding an accident. The physical world provides us with feedback, often immediate, about what is relevant and what is not.

Similarly, why do you turn on a light switch when you enter a dark room? When I ask this question, people often respond that they turn on a light "to see." Yes, obviously. But why do we want to see so badly? Because when we've walked through a darkened room, we've often enough hit something that's been painful to us. (No, this is not encouraging that kind of feedback to students. This is just a metaphor, sheesh!).

The point of these two examples is just to get us to realize that the physical environment provides frequent feedback when we fail to notice what is relevant. The problem is that the world of the classroom is abstract, made up of paper and images and so on—representations. If a student misses the "main idea" or "theme sentence" or a key operation in a math problem, the main idea won't jump out and stub his toe.

Relevant Facts First

Relevant Facts First!

Therefore, in HEQ, we follow a rule called "Relevant Facts First." This means that through our questioning, we try to get students to see the information in a way that stresses its importance. Most information has its own way of being understood, what I call its own "embedded order of relevancy." Even the layout of the written page, which is read from top to bottom, suggests that content on a page has its own embedded way of being examined. If we want the students to notice something first, then we should direct our questioning to that area, "What is at the top of the page?" If there is a key part of a problem that needs to be noticed, first, we might say, "Which mathematical operation do we start with in this expression?"

Noticing without relevancy:	Noticing with relevancy:

$$2 - 2 \times 2^2 =$$

$$2 - 2 \times 2^2 =$$

The rule of Relevant Facts First applies to all 7 Steps. As teachers, we often know what is relevant based upon our experience with a particular unit or problem or story. However, it can be helpful to establish what is relevant by asking ourselves three important questions before we begin questioning students:

- "How do I want this page to be noticed?"
- "How is the student likely to notice the page at first?"
- "How does the page suggest it wants to be noticed?"

Teaching Pitfalls

As teachers, we often have pre-existing patterns of doing things that may be different from the 7 Steps process. For instance, here in Step 1, when we ask students to label, identify or find the relevant facts first, this may require us to ask students about key terms or vocabulary. But in HEQ, we usually do not spend our time asking students too many questions about word meaning. This may sound heretical to some. While questions about word-meaning are important, they should not comprise the bulk of your Step 1 questions. I have observed lessons where a high proportion of the questions asked were, "And what does this word mean? And what does that word mean?"

Another pitfall is forgetting the rule of Relevant Facts First and allowing students to deliver irrelevant facts ad infinitum. If a student labels something that you do not feel is important to the problem or text, ask her to justify or tell why it is important, "Yes, that is a fact. Why do you feel it is important to the story?" This should obviously be done when students have given both relevant and irrelevant facts, as it is really a function of Q-R-Q.

Throughout Step 1 questioning, we hope to eventually change the students so that they naturally will come to look for the relevant information in a lesson. After a period of time, we should be able to turn to a student and say something like, "Please tell me the three key facts from the content" and the student would be able to say something like, "A, B and C are the key facts because of these reasons…" With enough training, it becomes normal for students to answer questions in whole expressions rather than bite-sizes answers or snippets of information. Labeling, though a lower level thinking skill, is truly critical to the next steps of the process of critical thinking.

Finally, a metaphor to help understand Step 1 follows. Consider the idea of asking students to identify or label the ingredients needed to make a cake. While you want students to notice all the ingredients, which one would you hope they notice, first? If the student notices the sprinkles, first, then perhaps their perception of what makes a cake is mostly decorative and not substantive. In Step 1, we hope the students will see the flour or sugar and then the other ingredients, labeling but doing so with a sense of priority.

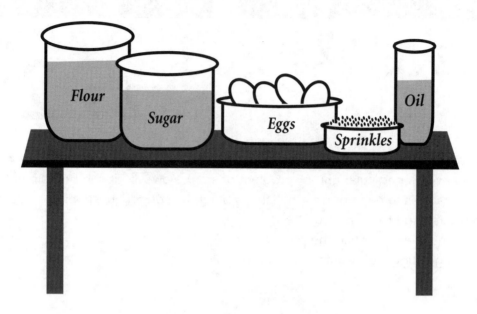

Ingredients Needed To Make A Cake

CHAPTER NINE:

STEP TWO

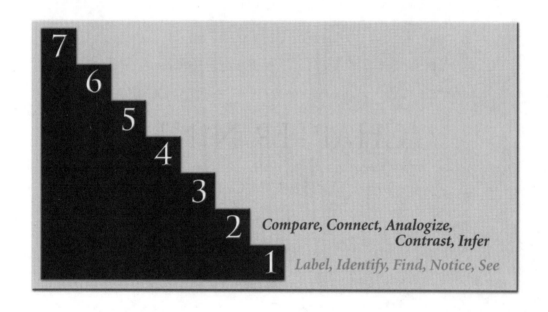

7
6
5
4
3
2   *Compare, Connect, Analogize,*
               Contrast, Infer
1   *Label, Identify, Find, Notice, See*

Step 2

The second step in our sequence of questioning is to ask students to connect, infer, compare, contrast and see disconnections in content. If Step 1 involves finding the relevant facts, then in Step 2 we are trying to make connections of and between those pieces of information.

In workshops, I've found that it pays to spend a moment talking about the language in Step 2. For instance, if I were to say that a gerbil lives in a cardboard box, and I asked, "What lives in the box?" the answer would of course be a gerbil. That relationship or connection between "gerbil" and "box" is a direct connection. Establishing such connections in terms of place, time, relationship, cause-effect and so on is what Step 2 is all about. What is the connection between A and B? How are things connected? How would you go from the first line in the problem to the second line?

Let's continue. If I were to say that a gerbil lives in a cardboard box, that gerbils have sharp teeth, and that a gerbil was placed in such a box and after an hour was nowhere to be found, what would one think? The gerbil chewed out of the box. This is an instance of inference.

Finally, if I were to say that a gerbil lives in a cardboard box, gerbils have sharp teeth, the gerbil was placed in the box and after an hour was nowhere to be found, and that therefore cats make the best kinds of pets, what would one think? In this case, there is a disconnection. The facts do not lead to the inference that cats make the best pets.

Getting students to notice where things are disconnected is very important. Often, we rightly focus on getting students to see connections in sets of information. This makes sense. Even small amounts of content, such as that contained by a paragraph, ostensibly are linked together in some way (hopefully so!).

However, students often fail to independently notice where information is missing, extra information is given, or things just don't make sense. In the search for connectivity or "meaning," sometimes, students overreach and forget to ask themselves, "Wait a minute. How does that make sense? I don't think it does!"

The benefits of asking students to notice where things are not connected properly come into play in different areas. In many written word problems in math, commonly there is given extra information that is not needed. If students are not asked to look at information with an eye towards both connection and disconnection, then they may believe everything given is relevant and must be used.

Another way of understanding the role of disconnection is to note that the incorrect answers on multiple-choice exam questions are in some way disconnected from either the question being asked or the given content. If A is the right answer, somehow B, C, and D must be disconnected from the specific inquiry or do not align with the content in some respect. We'll deal with how to use our oral questioning when working with written questions, like exam questions, in Steps 4 and 5, so there is no need to think too deeply about that now. But being aware of "disconnection" as a very important kind of question to ask will improve our Step 2 questions.

Step 2 questions can be used at the level of paragraphs to connect sentences to each other. They can be used between paragraphs. I often ask students to compare paragraphs, "What does this paragraph add or change from the previous paragraph?" This can be done at the level of pages or chapters, too.

And this can be done in math of course. How does the expression change from one line to the next? How are these problems alike or different? How can you go from step 1 to step 2, step 2 to step 3, step 3 to step 4, step 4 to step 5 and so on. It would be difficult to enumerate every possible Step 2 question. Indeed, the majority of questions we ask in the 7 Steps could be categorized as Step 2 questions.

There are two metaphors we can use to describe Step 2 questioning. One metaphor is that these questions help to develop a "conceptual web." As illustrated here, the multiplicity of connections between individual pieces of information can seem to form a web or star-like formation of information.

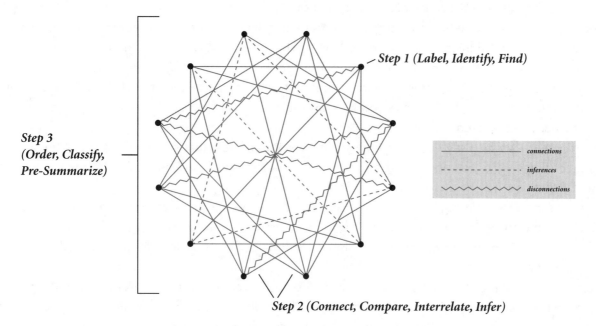

Another metaphor is to continue with our cake metaphor. In Step 2, we are asking students to mix ingredients and find connections. We might mix the liquids with each other and the solids with each other. On the other hand, we wouldn't want to mix the flour, sugar, and sprinkles all together. We see connections but recognize that not everything is always connected or should be combined all together.

By asking many Step 2 questions, we hope that eventually students will begin to naturally seek to make sense—to find connections and disconnections—between pieces of information. We would like to be able to simply ask the students, "Can you tell me several relevant connections or disconnections you found in your assignment?" and expect them to find those important relationships.

CHAPTER TEN:

STEP THREE

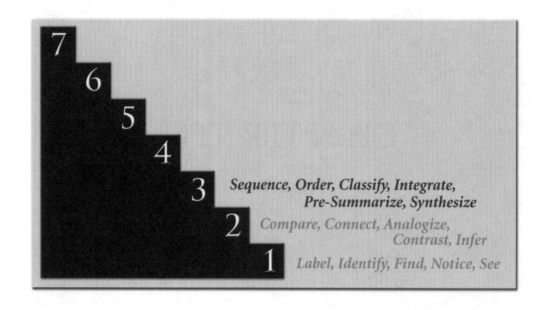

Sequence, Order, Classify, Integrate,
Pre-Summarize, Synthesize

Compare, Connect, Analogize,
Contrast, Infer

Label, Identify, Find, Notice, See

Step 3

Step 3 questions ask the student to integrate, put in order, classify or pre-summarize a set of facts or a portion of content. In HEQ, we use the word "pre-summarize" to mean a summary of a section of information. If a unit has 15 pages, we might ask a student to pre-summarize pages 1 to 5, then 6 to 10, and then 11-15 (same for steps in math problem or paragraphs on a page). I often call this an "interval summary" or "summarizing in chunks."

Sometimes, the term pre-summarize is thought to mean "summarizing something without looking at it in detail." For instance, I will hear teachers ask students to pre-summarize a story by looking at its title. Not to nitpick (okay, let's nitpick) but that sort of cognitive act is better described as an inference.

When asking students to pre-summarize, I often will say, "Can you tell it to me from beginning to end like a movie? Can you make it like a basketball game and tell me what happened in each quarter? Can you take me through several steps at a time?" So, in HEQ, to pre-summarize means to summarize in chunks.

Step 3 questions are very important. For one thing, of all the questions on state tests, I'd estimate that ¼ to 1/3 of test questions could be categorized as belonging to Step 3. When a question asks about a main idea, or asks for a summary, or asks what "comes next in the sequence," these are all questions that require the ability to summarize in chunks or put things in order.

Many students exhibit weakness when asked to respond to Step 3 kinds of questions. They have difficulty explaining an entire sequence of events or steps in solving a problem.

In terms of student responses to Step 3 questions, I look for three characteristics: completeness, order, and fluidity:

(1) Did the student include all the relevant items or points?

(2) Did they put them in order (if an order is warranted)?

(3) Were they fluid between the parts or in the retelling?

Sometimes, a student might tell you the all the relevant parts of a story on a page but then recount it in a way that develops out of order: "Yeah, so then, he developed three theories of how galaxies were formed and, um, he was then given an award. He also became a scientist." Wait, how'd he develop those theories and then become a scientist? You have to listen carefully to how students put things together in Step 3.

Fluidity means, does the student seem to transition logically or smoothly between the parts? Let's think about this metaphorically. Imagine that the players on a basketball team are able to run a play in its entirety but between each movement sort of get stuck and then, erratically, move to the next part of the play. Player A quickly passes the ball to Player B, who then holds it for a long time and then suddenly passes to Player C. Because of the time delay, however, the defensive player assigned to C is able to block his movement. The play is unsuccessful.

Sometimes, students can list all the steps of a problem but they can only do so in slow motion. Now, that can be a good starting point—let's walk through the play, first. If we get the basic movements right, we can learn to speed things up. But when students continue to move slowly and are never encouraged to go faster, they can get used to going at a slow speed. Thus, like the slow-moving basketball team, they have great plays but their execution never leads to a basket. Fluidity is very important to successfully hurdling this cognitive act.

I have found there to be two interrelated impediments to asking Step 3 questions in the classroom and, oddly enough, the issues are mostly cultural rather than cognitive in nature. What would prevent or inhibit us from asking a student, "Okay, so, tell me what you learned in Chapter 1 from beginning to end?"

The first problem is that teachers often fail to ask for whole summaries. Imagine a 5-step math problem. The teacher will say, "Julio, tell me step 1 of the problem. Sarah, what is step 2? Jim, what is step 3? Luke, what is step 4? Marissa, what is step 5?" At the end of this line of questioning, it will seem like the students have integrated the whole problem. In fact, no single student has done any pre-summary. The problem has been parted-out. We've had five subcontractors do the work of one or maybe two contractors.

I think we often refrain or hesitate a bit from asking a single student to do more than one bit of something in order to ensure that all students have a moment to participate. In HEQ, we want all students to participate but, on the other hand, we must balance this with moments when individual students are called to enact more complete summaries of information.

The other reason is that the class often will tune out when a single student is asked to speak for 30, 60, or 90 seconds in a row. Students don't know how to listen to each other. As readers will know, later in college you often realize that hearing other students respond to a question can be more valuable than listening to the professor talk. In any event, if the class can inhibit a student's longer response, that's a big problem.

Thus, as teachers trying to enact Step 3 cognition, we are fighting against two trends, first, our own desire to reach all students and secondly, students' inability to listen to each other. I think the first issue is relatively easy to overcome. Just be sure to ask for whole summaries or whole sections of information in order. But getting students to listen to each other requires a significant change. We must demand and not excuse when students fail to pay attention to each other. Otherwise, the cognitive acts of Step 3 will not occur for reasons of classroom culture rather than cognitive skill.

Sadly, rather than demanding that Step 3 occur and that student/group behavior comport to allow it to happen, many educators want to give in to classroom patterns that detract from it. Instead of saying, no, we must all listen to Maria and then Jim and then Raymond as each summarizes the story, we create other things for the disinterested students to do. At times, individualizing instruction in the interests of improving individual learning may detract from it because it forecloses important opportunities to hear other students talk and model their learning process. And students who cannot listen to others will find the world of group work to be a frustrating environment. Yes, I am talking about classrooms where a hundred things are going on at once supposedly to "reach every learner." Uh, then why are so few learners thus reached? Sometimes, to change from a bad habit, you've got to stop supporting the bad habit. This is rare insight, isn't it?

Steps 1 to 3

The first three of the 7 Steps help the student to go from a basic labeling of facts to the integration of entire sequences or processes. Another way of putting this is to go from the parts to the whole.

Steps 1, 2 & 3

Step 4

CHAPTER ELEVEN:

STEP FOUR

To me, none of these explanations convincingly explains things. If a question is "too simple," then why don't students say, "Ah, this is a really easy question. I've seen this fifty times. Basically, it's asking…" If they've never really seen such questions, then where have then been in the last few years? If they know it but can't say it, um, then how do we know they really know it?

I think the reason students have trouble telling us (and themselves) what written test questions ask is mostly due to the way we've led them to understand such test questions. Inadvertently, some teachers have taken over the role of interpreting or deconstructing test questions for students. Indeed, even as we ask oral questions to help students interpret written test questions, we may be creating some bad patterns. Before we go into detail in Step 4, let's look at the basic HEQ pattern in Step 4 and then compare that with other strategies educators may employ.

Read

HEQ	NON-HEQ	
Read *(the written-down question)*	**Read**	**Question:**
Interpret *(put in own words)*	**Step 1-***like* **(label key words)**	**When does the teacher**
Justify *(what was interpreted)*	**Step 2-***like* **(relate parts)**	**"intervene" in each**
Step 1-*like*	**Step 3-***like* **(classify question)**	**sequence?**
Step 2-*like*	**Interpret**	**Which pattern may**
Step 3-*like*	**Justify**	**increase dependency?**

The basic pattern in Step 4 is as follows: First, have students READ the actual question aloud. Yes, they can do this silently but reading aloud often helps both the student doing the actual reading and other students (ELL) to better hear what the question is asking.

Also, reading the question aloud helps us eliminate a common intuition about why a student does not understand a test question. Often, when a student misinterprets a written test question, teachers will become confused and ask the student to "Read it again!" They will explain that the student didn't actually "read" the question in the first place. But if the student has read the question aloud, how can it be that he didn't "read" it?

The "Read it again" strategy is used, I think, as a way of dealing with our own fear that perhaps the student in fact can read, but shockingly still doesn't understand. It's easier to believe that the student just didn't read it. Many students can speak words—make nice sounds—but not know of which they are speaking.

I admit that sometimes a second reading can give the student some new intuition about what a written question asks, but then why not establish this pattern for everything, including the content? Read it not once, but twice or three times! Why not sixteen times? And why do we, as teachers, only ask them to "Read it again" when they have misinterpreted a question as opposed to in all instances? Fundamentally, is the problem in "reading" or in some aspect of comprehension that goes beyond sound-making?

Quick story: I once had a problem with my cell phone. I called up my cellular company and said that I was having a problem with my cell phone. The technical representative said, "Do you have the manual for the phone?" Yes, I answered. "And did you read the section on…?" Yes, I said. Then, the representative had this unique insight that I could never have imagined. He said, "Okay, can you read it, again?"

So, as a first sub-step in Step 4, have the student read the written test question aloud.

Interpret

The second sub-step of Step 4 is to ask the student to INTERPRET the question. Simply say, "What does the question ask?" A common misstep here is to skip interpretation entirely. A teacher will ask the students to read a given question and then go immediately to the set of given answers (if multiple-choice). Skipping interpretation obviously reinforces a bad strategy for working with test questions and answers. And be careful that students simply don't repeat the written question word for word. This is not interpreting the question.

When I say that the student should interpret the question, this is often said to be asking the student to put the question "into his or her own words." That is, to transcribe the academic language of the written question into more common language. Be careful here, because students have learned to simply replace some of the words in the question with similar words but without really knowing what the question is asking. I call this analog replacement.

Consider the following transcription of the interpretation of a test question and the idea of analog replacement.

Me: Can you please read the question?
Student: What is the main idea of the passage?
Me: And could you interpret the question for me?
Student: It's asking for the main idea.
Me: And what's that?
Student: It's what it's all about.
Me: And how do you know what it's all about?
Student: It's like a summary of the whole thing.
Me: And what's a summary?
Student: It's the main point.

The conversation above shows students equating the main idea with a "what it's all about" or the "main point" or the "whole thing." These are common segments of language used to describe the concept of main idea. But what the student doesn't tell us is how to establish what a main idea is, the relationship between an overarching idea and a subordinate set of supporting facts or statements.

So, be sure students truly understand what the question is asking. Changing the language of a question is not in itself sufficient. The student must convey a sense of understanding the process of answering the question.

Justify

The third sub-step of Step 4 asks the student to JUSTIFY her interpretation of the question. This should occur whether or not the student has interpreted the question accurately or inaccurately. If the previous sub-step of interpretation asks, "What is the question asking?" then this sub-step asks, "And how do you know that is what the question is asking?"

We must recognize that sometimes a student will combine the process of interpretation and justification in one statement. He'll say, "The question is asking us to do X, because it says Y…" But a common mistake at this stage is skipping justification (of the interpretation) altogether. The student will say, "The question is ask-

Another pattern I've seen is this:
1. Read
2. Classify
3. Answer

In this pattern, the teacher asks the student to read the question. Then, the teacher asks, "What kind of question is this?" This question asks the student to classify the underlying question into one of several different categories, such as "opinion questions" or "main idea questions" and so on. Then, the student is asked to select an answer.

This second pattern is difficult for underachieving students to enact because it seeks a higher order thinking skill (classification of the question) based on archetypes (main ideas, opinions, causation, themes, sequences — concepts, really) as the initial step. It skips the interpretation of the question wherein the student is asked to frame the question in natural language.

The two aforementioned question-decoding strategies may be effective in select contexts. Both patterns can get the student to understand a given written question. But in HEQ, we believe the RIJ123 pattern of questioning is the most stable pattern for encouraging that students put initial effort into understanding the question and provide a framework for helping students when the get "stuck" with a particular question.

CHAPTER TWELVE:

STEP FIVE

considered a strong use of elimination strategies. Still, without any reasoning for selecting a particular answer as correct, the odds are 50% or, again, an F if probability alone is the guide.

If elimination strategies are not a particularly efficient way of analyzing multiple-choice answers, why are they so prominent in the educational landscape? The first reason is that for many state tests, the raw score needed to pass the exam may be less than 50% of the questions provided. (Hello, my un-named Mid-Atlantic state.) The raw score needed to pass most sections of state tests is usually between 30% and 65% of the items. In this easy-grading scenario, elimination strategies can be effective.

Another reason that elimination strategies are seen to be helpful is that they often require less reasoning ability to implement. Consider the following set of answers:

A. .5
B. 5
C. -.5
D. 100

Even when the question is not provided, as here, an examination of the answers suggests that answer D is too far afield to be correct. I call this kind of answer the "banana answer," as in, "Why is there a banana in my coffee?"

But the wider trend seems to be for state exams to become more difficult as time goes on until true grade level standards are set. There are different ways to make exams harder or easier. One way for exams to become harder is to require the content to match the grade level of the students. A 10th grade exam will become a real 10th grade exam using 10th grade content, not what is probably an 8th grade exam being given to 10th graders.

The other way for the exam to become more difficult is to make the answers closer to each other and thus require more reasoning to discern the correct one. Examine the answer sets below and see if you can tell what is happening:

A. -5	A. -5	A. -5
B. 5	B. 5	B. 5
C. -.5	C. -.5	C. -.5
D. 100	D. .05	D. .05
		E. A and B but not C

As you can see, when answers become "closer" together or more complicated, elimination strategies become less useful as a strategy for selecting a correct answer. Step 5 for HEQ is perhaps the "cleanest" approach. Simply ask the student, "What answer do you think correctly answers the question, and why do you think it does that?"

As a side note, when I think of elimination strategies I always think of a superintendent who I asked about the best route to return to the local airport. When I asked him how to get to the airport, he replied, "You could take route A, but that won't get you there in time. You could take route B, but you'd have to be a local to know how to get there. You could take route C, but you might get lost" and kept going on like that. I began to wonder, is there any route that will get me back to the airport? He eliminated all my choices! Do I hear a banjo in the distance?

Strategies for Working with Incorrect Answers

If a student has selected a correct answer and is able to provide justification for it, you may move to the next question or examine the other, incorrect answers to discern their flaws. But what if the student selects an incorrect answer in the first place? Of course, you ask them to justify that selection as you would if they had selected the correct answer. Still, what if they cannot figure out that the selected answer is not justifiable? Consider the following example:

Teacher: What answer do you think is correct?
Student: I think it's A.
Teacher: And why do you select A?
Student: Because it's right.
Teacher: And what makes it right?
Student: Um, I don't know. It just seems better.

To understand what to do at this point, we have to take a moment and consider what makes an answer "wrong" or incorrect in the first place (in general terms). Then, we can consider how to use oral questioning to guide the student to a better understanding.

In a multiple-choice set of answers, an answer that is incorrect is possibly (1) disconnected from the question being asked; (2) contains something missing from the content; (3) is missing something contained in the content.

Let's look at the first possibility. If the question asks for a "main idea" but the answer selected by the student is only a detail, then the answer is divorced from the question. This kind of error is really an error that must have occurred in Step 4. But what if the student has, in fact, properly understood the question but still has selected an incorrect answer? In this case, the second and third situations may apply.

In the second situation, the answer selected includes information not given in the content. Consider the following text:

Many of the new fruits imported into our country come from abroad. These fruits are grown in tropical climates. Mangoes, bananas, cantaloupes and guava are examples of imported tropical fruit. People like them because they taste sweet and are now affordable to the average person due to fast transportation from overseas.

Q. Which of the following statements is supported by the text?

I. A mango is an imported fruit.	A. I
II. Taste is the key to affordable fruit.	B. II and IV
III. Pineapples are an imported fruit.	C. III
IV. Quick transport keeps cantaloupes fresh.	D. III and IV

Assume the student selects C. This answer contains something that is not mentioned by the given text.

Teacher: Yes, that is true. What else is in the text?

Student: Um, something about transparency.

Teacher: And what else?

Student: Natural resources.

Teacher: So, all these things you mentioned—natural resources, transparency, education, institutions—are those contained in answer C? If so, where or how?

Of course things might not work out perfectly from here. But the point is to show that the teacher asks questions to develop the content and then compares that to the answer initially selected by the student. This is called going from "content to answer" in Step 5. It is a good strategy when there is information missing from the selected answer that is contained in the text or given information.

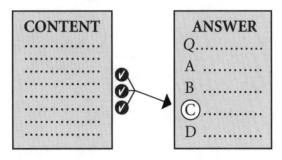

What is in the problem? Are those in "C"?

Both the answer-to-content and content-to-answer strategies illustrate what I call the direction of questions. Do you start at the answer choice and then go to the content or vice versa? While by no means are these fool-proof strategies for getting students to self-correct, they do give us some insight into how we might use oral questions to help students come to a better understanding.

Step 5 of HEQ is very simply at heart. Simply ask students to justify any answer the select. Always try to get them to go for the "right" answer if they can. Avoid using elimination strategies as a first strategy. And use either the answer-to-content or content-to-answer strategies when a student has selected an incorrect answer.

CHAPTER THIRTEEN:

STEP SIX

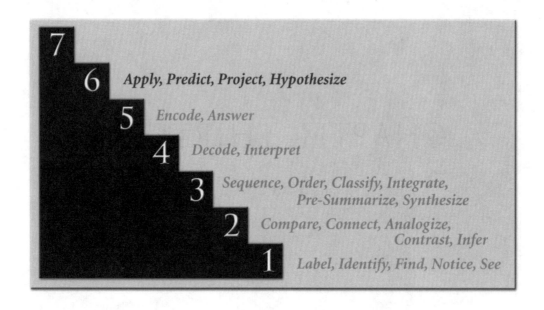

7

6 *Apply, Predict, Project, Hypothesize*

5 *Encode, Answer*

4 *Decode, Interpret*

3 *Sequence, Order, Classify, Integrate,
Pre-Summarize, Synthesize*

2 *Compare, Connect, Analogize,
Contrast, Infer*

1 *Label, Identify, Find, Notice, See*

Step 6

Step 6 is to ask students to apply, predict, change, or use what has been learned in the lesson in some new or different context. Some samples of Step 6 questions, include:

- How would you use this in another context
- How would you apply this information to your own life?
- If you double each variable, how will this affect the problem?
- What if this had never happened?
- Can you predict what might happen if?

Step 6 questions are easy to ask. As adults, we are often interested in how our content applies to our own lives or has impacted our present condition. How might we use this learning? If Step 6 questions are inherently appealing for adults to engage, then why are these kinds of questions troublesome for some students? Again, asking Step 6 kinds of questions without a strong foundation in other steps lends to prediction without under-standing—speculation. Thus, as much as adults find these questions easy to ask, we must set up the foundation for Step 6 in the other preceding steps.

There is a minor issue of semantics that arises in Step 6. Sometimes, people confuse the concept of infer-ence (from Step 2) with that of prediction (from Step 6). For instance, if I were to say that a car was going too fast and took a swerve around a bend in the road, and then we heard the sounds of a crash, we would "infer" that there had been an accident or collision. As the crash must have already taken place, there is nothing left to predict. If, on the other hand, we saw the same car go around the bend and saw another car coming in the opposite direction, we might "predict" a crash. Perhaps the difference between an inference and a prediction is that a prediction requires some change in the given information, something to happen in the future, not what has already occurred.

Step 6 questions are intended to help the student see the utility or relevance of what they learned in pre-vious steps. You may, at your discretion, allow students who are capable of answering Step 6 questions make efforts at asking such questions to other students.

CHAPTER FOURTEEN:

STEP SEVEN

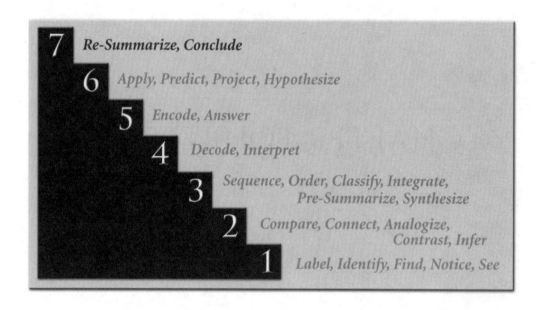

7 Re-Summarize, Conclude

6 Apply, Predict, Project, Hypothesize

5 Encode, Answer

4 Decode, Interpret

3 Sequence, Order, Classify, Integrate,
Pre-Summarize, Synthesize

2 Compare, Connect, Analogize,
Contrast, Infer

1 Label, Identify, Find, Notice, See

Step 7

Step 7 asks students to do a final summary of what they learned in the lesson or unit or class period. Step 7 may be initiated simply by asking students, "What did you learn today?" You should hope that students mix and match between key facts, connections, summaries and applications. The goal of Step 7 is both to summarize the given content but also to enable students to see the connectedness between days and weeks.

Often, teachers do the job of summarizing for students, particularly at the end of a class period. The teacher will say, "Okay, today we did X, Y, and Z. For tomorrow, I'd like…" While time pressures may sometimes require the teacher to give the summary, in HEQ we vastly prefer for students to tell what it is they learned. Again, call on two or three students and ask, "What did you learn?"

It is often noticed that Step 7 is really like Step 3 in the sense of putting things together as a whole, an integration of sorts. The difference between Step 3 and Step 7 is the intervening steps, where the student hopefully learns something new from assessment questions and the application of what was learned (Steps 4, 5, and 6).

One strategy that I have seen used is to ask students to do an exercise called, "I learned." Each student is asked to complete the sentence without repeating what the previous student learned. This may also help students when they go home and are asked, "What did you do in school today?"

CHAPTER FIFTEEN:

COMMON QUESTIONS

Common Questions

Let's talk common questions educators have when looking at HEQ for the first time.

Must I "exhaust" the cognitive acts of one step before moving on to the next step? That is, should I ask my students to "label" everything before I ask them even a single question that might elicit a comparison? The answer is no. You only need to ask students a few questions in a particular step before making a decision that students might be ready to do the next kind of thinking. And so on.

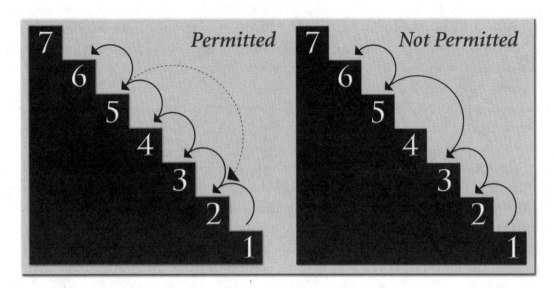

Can you go back to a previous step or kind of question if a student seems to need to be asked something? For instance, if I ask a student to make an inference (Step 2) and then she seems to have forgotten a key piece of information necessary for that inference, could I ask her to identify (Step 1) that that missing piece? Yes, you may go back to previous steps as needed to make the lesson continue to move forward. If you want to think in terms of the cognitive scaffold, you may continue to reinforce the lower levels of the scaffold but remember that you want to keep building it up, too.

It is not wise to skip entire categories of questioning; we should not skip a step of questioning. Why not? Logically, each step lays the foundation for the next step. Labeling (Step 1) gives us something to compare (Step 2). Comparison gives us the connections needed to make sequences or see the whole of something (Step 3). So, skipping steps is not a good idea at all.

Does HEQ allow for the teacher to give a piece of information, ever? Yes. While HEQ uses questioning as the primary modality or way of teaching, sometimes it is just quicker and doesn't hurt things to give a piece of information to a student. HEQ, therefore, is not "pure" questioning but mostly pure questioning. See? I hope so.

Another question I am sometimes asked is, "Can I ever give students the answer to a question?" Um, then why ask it? Okay, to be fair, I do understand that sometimes the bell is about to ring and it's important that all students recognize that, bottom line, answer C, gorilla, is not the name of a Founding Father. So, tell what you must. But try to keep the mode in a questioning format, when you can. An all too common sight is of teachers asking good questions and then answering their own questions! It's as if I were to say to a class of students, "The next question is for my very best student. Oh, that would be me." Let's try not to answer our own questions.

What happens if I ask a bad question? Can I retract a question? Sure. On many occasions, I'll catch myself midway through asking a bad question where I jumble my words or it sounds confusing and I'll say, "Scratch that. Okay, here's the question…" Students appreciate it when you can admit something is poorly asked.

Can students do the asking of questions to each other? That would be great. But if you've been reading this book, by now you probably agree that questioning is not entirely a simple thing to do, properly. Anybody can "ask questions," but do they know why they are asking questions, how questions are structured, why questions are important for reasoning development and how so? Being able to answer these questions involves some "metacognition" about the nature of questioning. Many students are not particularly fluid at the cognitive acts initiated by questions, so asking them to be metacognitive about the entire questioning process puts the horse before the cart, so to speak.

On the other hand, it probably does no great harm—though not great good--for students to ask each other questions. My suggestion is this: If students are answering your own questions successfully, then you may go ahead and let them ask each other questions and see how it goes. But until they can do that, asking them to ask each other questions is like saying, "I'm not having any luck with you. Why don't you try it with each other?" Abandon ship! Abandon ship! Thus, strategies like "pair/share" are not a part of HEQ. This doesn't mean you can't use them. Use them when you make a judgment they will work. This is another reason why HEQ isn't a true program; it doesn't prohibit practices that contrast with it.

What about ELL/ESL students? Obviously, students with no knowledge of English can have a question translated (if available) but most ELL students have some command of English, usually more than we think. Still, there is no perfect answer about how to question students who are both learning English and trying to learn at the same time.

Questioning the ELL student, even when imperfect, is beneficial for at least two reasons unique to the asking of questions. First, the format and tempo of questions is different than a stream of words in a lecture. Questions have the advantages that they are spaced out to give students time to think and respond, in addition to allowing the ELL student to hear how other students may put things. Secondly, asking questions to the ELL student sends the message that, "Your participation is important to me" which lecture may not do.

This idea of the engagement aspect to questioning for the ELL student cannot be overemphasized. Consider this thought experiment: In situation A, you are placed in a room with a television and foreign language programming and must listen to that for 8 hours a day. In situation B, you are put in the foreign country to walk around for 8 hours a day. In both situations, you hear nothing but the foreign language. But where would you learn the language quickest? I think the reason it is easier to learn in the foreign country is that the engagement is forced upon you by the need to communicate. If you never spoke to anyone when walking around, you'd be back in situation A. For the ELL student, HEQ is more like environment B because it forces that engagement to happen.

What about inclusion classrooms? Well, yes, it's harder to ask questions in an inclusion setting where students might be all over the board in terms of their cognitive development. But the same is true for lecture. And what about students who have individual education plans (IEP)? Teachers have told me that some IEPs have even prohibited asking a student a question! Well, follow the law or plan as required. (Note to self: Don't break the law).

What about moving on if a student doesn't understand or is not able to answer a question after a few attempts? This is simply a fact of life. You can't spend all day trying to bring a single student to understanding. The other students will probably get out of control if you try to do that. You can always come back to that student at a later time with other questions or assistance.

Is this the most satisfying answer? No. But the reality is that we "move on" all the time in our classrooms with imperfect understanding. The difference is that during lecture or individual study we often get to gloss over the fact that many students do not understand. We just don't hear about it until an exam or quiz is taken. What HEQ through its oral questioning forces us to do, is realize that we normally move on when the majority of students can answer our questions, knowing that some students just aren't where we'd want them to be. As teachers, this is often troubling to us. But, again, in lecture we cover this reality up, often by occasionally asking, "Okay, do you understand this?" and students usually assent, making us feel better but we all know the question is mostly rhetorical. With HEQ, at least we all know where we stand at a given moment—who, and how many, know what.

How long does HEQ questioning last? For younger grades, using HEQ might extend for 5 minutes to perhaps 10 consecutive minutes in length. Those little ones have trouble sitting through lots of questions in a row. Gradually, as the grades go up, we make the questioning more intensive. A 7th grade class might be able to do 20 minutes of HEQ. An 11th grade class might go for 30 minutes in HEQ. Don't forget that HEQ is also tiring for the teacher. So, moderate your time in questioning. You don't have to complete all 7 Steps of questioning in a single class period. You can split things up, say, Steps 1 to 3 for today and 4 to 7 for tomorrow, if that makes sense.

I am sometimes told that "research" says that going more than 20 minutes in one kind of teaching style isn't "good for learning." Hmm, I'd be surprised that cognitive research says as much as that in a definitive way. But that may be the case in some subject areas or with certain students.

On the other hand, consider what life requires, which is often concentrated learning or effort directed at something for more, much more, than 20 minutes. This is not to say go for 60 minutes of questioning! But aren't we exacerbating that which we'd like to reduce when we constantly are shifting instructional techniques to "reach all students?" If ADHD or ADD or whatever a lack of attention will eventually be abbreviated as is ascendant, is it possible it is because of our schoolwide efforts to accommodate rather than resist it? I don't know the answer, but it's a question that I ask myself. Well, for HEQ, we normally don't go beyond 30-35 minutes of questioning at the high school level, anyway.

How will students feel if they can't answer a question? Won't they feel unsuccessful? In HEQ, there is no perfection to the process of either asking questions or students constructing answers. Indeed, as our questions must always be leading students to new learning, we will always be in circumstances where many of our questions are not answered exactly right. I'd estimate up to 1/3rd of the questions we ask might not result in precisely what we'd like to hear and the lesson may still be going very well. To encourage learning, we must risk failure in both the questions we ask and the responses students may give us.

This idea that successful learning may require asking questions that don't lead to immediate success or reward is counterintuitive to some. Innately, many of us want to hear our students give the "right answer" and reward them for that. Being able to tell a student he or she is "successful" also allows us to tell ourselves that, if the student is successful, the teacher must also be doing something right. Sadly, promoting a culture of "successful learners" often contrasts with the process that actually leads to success for most students—effort.

How do students respond to HEQ strategies? How do they respond to all that questioning? Getting used to HEQ by students may be compared to the first time drivers get on the highway or freeway. The first time I entered a freeway, I can remember feeling a bit nervous to be driving so fast with cars all around. After a bit of experience, it was no problem. Okay, I still worry about crazy drivers but the point is that a "highway of questioning" or high levels of student engagement via questioning just takes some getting used to, that's all. And once you are used to it, you never think about it again. When engagement is common, disengagement is what becomes bothersome.

Is it helpful to write out the questions in advance? In HEQ, we often plan out a few questions at each of the steps as guideposts for our lesson. We try to move the lesson in the direction of those questions. Those written-out questions are also helpful if we lose our track in asking questions and need a reminder of what to ask. I find that when people actually write out their questions, they have a better tendency to actually ask them, too. Of course, you don't have to write out every single question you might ask in a lesson. Think of the written questions as waypoints on a long journey. You don't plan each mile of the trip, but you might keep in mind key cities as places you need to pass.

CHAPTER SIXTEEN:

CONCLUSION

I have dedicated the last ten years to providing educators with a substantive yet practical approach to the use of questioning strategies in the K-12 classroom. For many of those years, I focused on which strategies would prove effective in classrooms. During HEQ workshops, we always have demonstrated with students as a part of each inservice, giving us the opportunity to try strategies out.

What I have realized is that the technical aspects of questioning—which this book hopefully addresses—is not the key to effective questioning. Rather, it is the culture of the classroom, of the school, of teachers and students and parents that makes the difference between engaging classrooms and sullen streams of lecture or worksheets. In short, effective questioning is mostly about attitude.

Are we, as American educators, will to challenge our students not with platitudes but with direct and systematic questions to develop their intelligence and improve their engagement? Are we willing to say that it is unacceptable to just sit there? Effective questioning is not rocket science; it can be done. But it will require a big change in attitude and behavior by everyone involved in schools.

I believe questioning helps to develop cognitive skill. But the future is one of incredible cognitive competition. Cognition—being smart—may become a commodity in many respects. To succeed, then, we'll need more than intelligence. Our students will need an attitude of engagement that will distinguish them from the literally tens or hundreds of millions of technically capable, smart people out there in the wide world.

In short, in my eyes, HEQ is mostly about challenging the culture of disengagement found in many classrooms and schools. But the culture of disengagement will not be defeated in a single period. It will take persistent years of effort to overcome the passivity inured in some students like dried clay. Fortunately, HEQ is a tool in the arsenal, a quiver to unleash some questions at students and see what happens.

I know—I do—that we can do this and create engagement through questioning and other pedagogical strategies. But it is a question of will. One way or another, I know that I'll be asking questions. Best of luck in your own effective questioning of students.

Yours,

Ivan Hannel, J.D.
Author, HEQ
Phoenix, AZ, USA
May 2006
www.hannel.com

INDEX
OF IMAGES

Image 1.1; Page 9

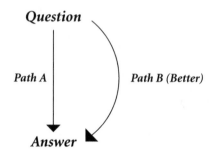

Image 2.1; Page 15

Image 2.2; Page 18

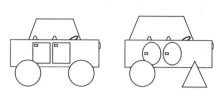

Image 4.1; Page 25

Image 4.2; Page 26

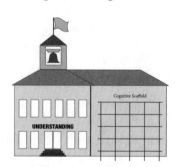

Image 5.1; Page 37

Image 6.1; Page 47

Image 6.2; Page 47

Image 6.3; Page 48

Image 6.4; Page 48

Image 6.5; Page 50

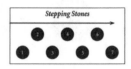

Image 8.1; Page 61

Image 8.2; Page 62

Image 8.3; Page 63

Image 8.4; Page 64

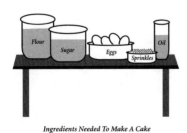

Image 9.1; Page 68

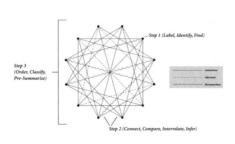

Image 9.2; Page 68

INDEX OF IMAGES

Image 10.1; Page 72

Image 11.1; Page 78

HEQ	NON-HEQ
Read *(the written-down question)*	Read
Interpret *(put in own words)*	Step 1-*like* (label key words)
Justify *(what was interpreted)*	Step 2-*like* (relate parts)
Step 1-*like*	Step 3-*like* (classify question)
Step 2-*like*	Interpret
Step 3-*like*	Justify

Question:
When does the teacher "intervene" in each sequence? Which pattern may increase dependency?

Image 12.1; Page 85

Test Question

Answer Set #1	Answer Set #2	Answer Set #3
A. -5	A. -5	A. -5
B. -.05	B. -.05	B. -.05
C. 5	C. 5	C. 5
D. -.5	D. -.5	D. -.5
Eliminating One Answer Choice	*Eliminating Two Answer Choices*	*Eliminating Three Answer Choices*

Image 12.2; Page 88

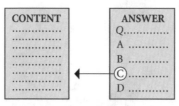

Is "C" in the problem?

Image 12.3; Page 89

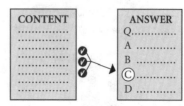

What is in the problem? Are those in "C"?

Image 15.1; Page 101

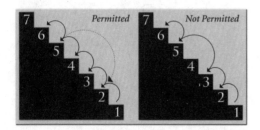